GUIDE TO SHORT FILMS

GUIDE TO SHORT FILMS

JEFFREY SCHRANK

HAYDEN BOOK COMPANY, INC.
Rochelle Park, New Jersey

ISBN   0-8104-6035-1
Library of Congress Catalog Card Number   78-24701

                              Printed in the United States of America

        1   2   3   4   5   6   7   8   9   PRINTING

        79 80 81 82 83 84 85 86 87   YEAR

INTRODUCTION

Guide to Short Films is a guide to 228 of the most creative, educational, and entertaining short films currently available for sale and rental. The films described in this book are rarely the sort that are commonly called "instructional films," nor are they the type often called "experimental" or "underground." The films were created neither to fill a need in the school curriculum nor to experiment with a new camera technique. Rather, they are the creations of individual artists, craftspeople, and communicators working more often out of love for film or a vital interest in the subject matter than for personal gain.

Rental of Films

All the films described here are available for rental from the company or companies listed at the end of each review. Addresses are provided at the end of the book. A film described as "From . . ." can be purchased or rented from the source given. "Rental from . . ." means that the source listed will only rent the film and not sell it.

The film libraries of the University of California at Berkeley and the University of Michigan are listed as rental sources. Many other university libraries (notably Minnesota and Kent State) have large collections and will provide service anywhere in the country. A university library will usually be the least expensive rental source, but university libraries have a limited number of prints (often only a single copy) to distribute and are therefore least able to accommodate specific dates. The original distributor of a film will usually provide the best quality prints and the most flexible service. Those renting films on a limited budget should try university film libraries as well as the film collections maintained in many large public libraries.

Viewfinders is an often-listed source of film rentals. They charge the same rental as the original distributor and provide good quality prints, flexible booking dates, and personalized service. They serve as a kind of film rental "travel agent," able to book films from a wide variety of other film distributors.

Prices

No prices are given in this book since they are highly changeable. Short films rent from $10 to $50 per showing. The longer the film, the higher the rental fee is likely to be. A few longer films described here rent for more than $50. Using university film libraries will save from 20 to 50 percent in rental fees.

Films can also be purchased, with prices starting slightly under $100 (for very short films) and going to well over $500. Many of the distributors also will sell prints of their films in 3/4 inch, U-Matic videocassette format.

Using Films

The films described in this book are as diverse as possible. In addition to their use in schools, short films are ideal for:

- Discussion sparking
- Alternatives to lectures and speakers (a film rental is less than a speaking fee, and a film is often more involving than a lecture)
- Do-it-yourself film festivals
- Parties
- Fund-raising gatherings
- Business and management training programs
- Retreats
- Group therapy or counseling sessions
- Public meetings
- Group discussions or consciousness-raising sessions
- Alternatives to television

Using This Book

Films are arranged in alphabetical order. To locate films on specific topics, use the Subject Index, which has been designed to be used like a thesaurus. It is intended to suggest creative combinations of films and ideas.

Many of the film descriptions in this book first appeared in slightly different form in *Media Mix Newsletter*. The continuing reviews in *Media Mix* serve as a convenient update to this collection. Subscriptions are available from *Media Mix*, 21 West Madison Street, Chicago, IL 60606.

All films described in this book were screened before being included. Most were made in the 1970s. No claim is made that these films are the best available. Many well-known older films are not included since they have been adequately described in other publications.

Getting Started

Those readers who have never rented films will find the process simple. Contact the distributor listed for the film you wish to rent and supply the date (and two alternate dates if possible) on which you wish to show the film. The distributor will either send you a confirmation or will inform you that the film is booked for those dates.

New customers not using institutional purchase orders may have to pay in advance. Distributors supply instructions telling how to return films after use.

Commercial distributors offer free catalogs. Write or call, using the addresses given on pages 183-185. University libraries sometimes charge a fee for their catalogs. A good "first catalog" for the beginner at film rental is the free one from Viewfinders, Box 1665, Evanston, IL 60204.

CONTENTS

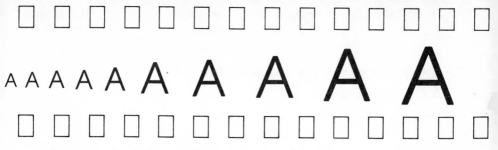

Abel Gance: The Charm of Dynamite

Abel Gance is a French filmmaker of the 1920s whose name is often mentioned in cinema history courses as the originator of the panoramic screen. But little more is said of the man, mainly because very few Americans have ever seen a Gance film. Historian Kevin Brownlow has studied the works of Gance and has compiled a film which argues forcefully that Gance ranks with Eric von Stroheim, Orson Welles, and even Sergei Eisenstein as a genius-maverick and seminal figure in film history. Gance was still alive in the late 1960s and at last received some recognition in France.

In the 1920s, Gance was making films using a hand-held camera, a dolly, and crude moving booms, multiple split screens, and fast cutting that makes Charles Braverman look like a copycat. Gance experimented with cameras slung on an overhead cable and even a pendulum, as well as with 3-D and color.

Abel Gance: The Charm of Dynamite uses film clips from *Napoleon*, *La Roue*, and *J'Accuse* to show the genius of a filmmaker far ahead of his time. In one sequence shot from the rear of a moving train, Gance allows the patterns of the railroad tracks to play a visual symphony of lines much as Norman McLaren did 30 years later by drawing directly on film. Even Sergei Eisenstein gave credit to Gance and studied his works for ideas. What is today often called Russian montage should perhaps be credited as much to Gance as to the better-known group of Russian directors.

Gance is interviewed during this film and speaks of his desire to use the power of cinema to show the stupidity of war. To Gance, "Enthusiasm is everything; it is impossible to make a great film without it."

Abel Gance: The Charm of Dynamite is a reminder that film is still a young art and that its history needs revision and rediscovery. Anyone who studies or teaches film history should be familiar with the work of Abel Gance, and this film serves as an excellent introduction. For further study, Gance's films are being restored and released in the United States by Images. Now available are *Bonaparte et la Revolution* (a lengthy 254 minutes, made back in 1925) and *J'Accuse*, a sound feature made in 1937.

52 minutes, color and black and white, directed by Kevin Brownlow, narrated by Lindsay Anderson (1968). From Images.

Afternoons and Alice McClure: A Child's Fantasy

"Things can be real if you want them to be," little Alice tells her diary. This Alice has a private wonderland, an abandoned Victorian house boarded and waiting for the wreckers. Alice looks at the house lovingly on her way to school one day and decides to investigate. The black-and-white film turns to a butterscotch color as she enters the house to make it real.

To Alice, the house is not an abandoned piece of real estate, but a domain where she can entertain guests in a grand style befitting its history. She cleans the dusty parlor and drags in cast-off furnishings supplied by a friendly junk dealer and a skid row alley. Once the house has been refurbished, she goes to a fruit market to buy food for her imagined banquet, and she greets the guests as they arrive.

Afternoons and Alice McClure captures a child's fantasy world in a realistic way. Some students find Alice ready for a psychiatrist, others feel sorry for her loneliness, while still others are moved by memories of their own long-dead fantasy worlds. *Afternoons* is a pleasant, relaxing film with more discussion possibilities than might at first appear. A nice companion piece for either *My Goat* or *The Open Window* for a comparison of youthful fantasies.

Note: This film is available in two versions. In one, subtitled, "A Child's Tragedy," Alice is killed by an intruder while at play. The murder is dramatically unsound and ruins what is otherwise a simple fantasy film.

28 minutes, color, directed by William J. Schwartz (1973). From Phoenix Films; rental also from Viewfinders.

Ain't Gonna Eat My Mind

This is a harrowing documentary trip down the "mean streets" of the South Bronx. Black Benjy, a member of the Ghetto Brothers, has been murdered by a rival gang, and retaliation fills the neighborhood. Producer/director Tony Batten interviews Charles Milendez, Ghetto Brothers president, and walks with him in an attempt to prevent further violence. A gathering of the "families" is called, and leaders of the Young Cobras, the Savage Skulls, the Nomads, and the Young Sinners put aside their guns and switchblades to talk. Their "raps" are street drama of the highest order—improvised, earthy, rhythmic, tough yet deeply personal. The meeting cools things off, at least for a while.

Ain't Gonna Eat My Mind continues with interviews with a junior high principal, a math teacher, youth workers, and gang members. The story they tell is compelling and one that street kids in any large city can readily understand. Suburban students will find this world hard to identify with, but at least they will realize that the ghetto offers more than crime and poverty. The film won a Du Pont—Columbia University Award and a 1973 New York State Emmy Award.

34 minutes, color. Sale from Carousel Films; rental from University of California.

America: Everything You've Ever Dreamed Of

This is a grouping of four short satires originally shown on the ill-fated *Great American Dream Machine* of PBS.

"The Best Years of Your Life" damns an Arizona retirement community with the praise of its own salesmen and its contented residents. To the tune of the development's theme song, "Wake Up and Live in Sun City," satisfied couples call their paradise "utopia," "America Beautiful," and "the greatest resort community in the world." One comments that "there are few liberals here, but it's basically an American community." This segment of the film, like the other three, is totally unfair, biased, and distorted, but it's a brilliant example of cinema satire.

"Honeymoon Hotel" takes out after the Pocono mountain honeymoon hotels offering heart-shaped bathtubs amid an atmosphere of plastic bliss. Again the couples praise their experience at Love Haven. "This place is just like a dream world; just like the dreams of a little girl."

The third segment of this film selects for its victim the Campus Crusade for Christ, while the final part takes on that standard audio wallpaper of the business world—Muzak.

25 minutes, color, directed by Rhoden, Streeter, and Ganz (1971). From Films, Inc.; rental also from Viewfinders and University of Michigan.

American Shoeshine

This film made its way through the labyrinthian mysteries of the nominating process for an Academy Award and emerged a winner. *American Shoeshine* is not a bad film; it is pleasing, mildly entertaining, and serves to document a substratum of Americana never before seen on film. Why *American Shoeshine* received an Oscar instead of the hundreds of other better-made and more perceptive short films created in 1975 is impossible to judge. The film certainly deserves recognition but does not represent the pinnacle of film art for any year.

American Shoeshine explores the world of the corner shoeshine stands and finds in them a reflection of American history, values, and psychology. The shoeshine stand has already become a near-relic. But once these humble enterprises of immigrants and blacks served as community gathering places, as some form of dignity in the face of otherwise certain unemployment, as substitute confessionals, and as the poor man's psychiatry couch. The decline of the shoeshine stand mirrors the development of institutions as society's preferred means of meeting human needs.

The film allows "bootblacks" to speak for themselves and even to demonstrate the lost art of the "rag jive"—the shoeshine as folk music. *American Shoeshine* is a northern, urban answer to the *Foxfire*-type films from the Appalachian area—a reminder that Americans need not be 80 years old and live in a mountain cabin to have a story to tell about folk history.

29 minutes, black and white, directed by Sparky Greene (1975). From Perspective Films; rental also from University of California.

Angel and Big Joe

This film won the 1975 Academy Award as the best live action short film. It is a part of the LCA "Learning to Be Human" series that also contains *The Boy Who Liked Deer* and *The Shopping Bag Lady*.

Angel and Big Joe stars Paul Sorvino as Big Joe, a recognizable face from a variety of TV and movie roles, and the likable Dadi Pinero as young Angel Diaz. The acting in *Angel and Big Joe* is some of the best I've seen in a short film, the direction is simple and flawless, and the script and story both entertaining and touching.

Angel is a Mexican/Puerto Rican youngster who has been a migrant worker all his life. Big Joe is a telephone repairman who fixes the pay phone Angel and his mother use occasionally to call the father who is off looking for a new crop to pick. Angel and Big Joe move from hesitant belligerence to deep friendship in the course of the film, and Angel is forced to make a decision between moving on with his family or staying with Big Joe as a combination adopted son and business partner. The film is excellent for a discussion of responsibility to self versus responsibility to one's family. But it is even better as an entertaining story of the progress of a relationship moving from mutual need to true friendship.

27 minutes, color, directed by Bert Salzman. From Learning Corporation of America; rental also from MMM.

Animation Pie

If I had to choose one film for students of any age below college level to excite them about filmmaking, it would probably be *Animation Pie*. The film shows kids at work (or is it play?) making flipbooks (which are then turned into films), films drawn directly on the celluloid, pixilation, cut-out animation, and clay animation. The film inspires viewers to make their own films and even gives some practical ideas on how to go about getting started in animation. There is no narration, and technical details are kept to a minimum.

Animation Pie will not make up for a teacher who does not know how to make films, but it will motivate students and give some practical ideas.

The film shows a few of the kids' animation extravaganzas—highly creative yet very kidlike. *Animation Pie* is far more practical and creative than *Life Times Nine*, more fun than *Animation: Frame by Frame*, and more varied than *How to Make Movies Without a Camera*.

The film's only weakness is that it tends to drag a bit toward the end by showing too many examples of student-made clay animation films.

25 minutes, color, directed by Robert Bloomberg. From Filmwright.

Antonia

When *Antonia* came out in 1974 to rave reviews, I could not understand why a film about Judy Collins's piano teacher should be anything more than a passing curiosity. *Time* ranked *Antonia* as one of the ten best films of the year, as did its irreverent counterpart, *New Times*. The New York critics used every word in their thesauruses to praise the film, and Hollywood nominated it for an Academy Award as the best feature-length documentary. Perhaps, I surmised, the reason for the acclaim is that this was a woman's film in a year when, as Chicago film critic Gene Siskel observed, "Critics are waiting to confer dollars and awards on virtually any film in which a woman talks in complete sentences and keeps her clothes on for most of the picture."

But the real reason for *Antonia*'s success becomes evident upon viewing; it is simply a carefully constructed documentary about a fascinating human being. *Antonia* can be profitably shown in any documentary, women's studies, or music education course, or in any situation where audiences appreciate fine films.

Antonia Brico was acclaimed at 28 as a great conductor. She impressed audiences the world over but received press raves that reduced her to a curiosity—"Cinderella to Lead Great Bowl Orchestra" or "Yankee Girl Startles German Critics." Today she conducts a nonprofit orchestra in Denver that manages to play five times a year and rehearses in a local Baptist church. Antonia is strong enough to conduct five concerts a month and finds the closed door a "perpetual heartbreak."

But *Antonia* is a film about a strong and sensitive woman, not about failure. It is about a woman who has received praise from the world's greatest musicians and has conducted in the world's most famous concert halls. *Antonia* is about a great teacher who survived an unhappy childhood ("the music was the thing that saved my sanity") and who took up the piano at age ten only because her doctor advised it as a way to stop fingernail biting.

Antonia spends much of her time teaching piano (the film never mentions that she taught Judy Collins) to talented young girls who might someday themselves become great pianists or conductors when the walls of sexism have fallen. *Antonia* captures the humanity of one person in a way few films do; and what more valuable role could film play than to present a human being accurately and lovingly?

58 minutes, color, directed by Jill Godmilow and Judy Collins (1974). From Phoenix Films.

Anything You Want to Be

This is not a review of Liane Brandon's useful little film about sexism called *Anything You Want to Be*. This is a review of a free-loan film, also on sexism, available from Bell Telephone offices, that unfortunately has the same title as the earlier Brandon effort. Someone at Bell didn't let their fingers do the walking through a film directory.

Anything You Want to Be is 28 minutes of snatches of interviews with people who do not fit common stereotypes of the work a man or a woman should do. Heard from in the film are a male typist who says, "I should be able to be a typist if I want to," a woman zookeeper, a male nursery school teacher, a woman cleric, a woman rabbi, a woman corporate executive. There are also a number of women shown working for AT&T in traditionally male roles and at least one male switchboard operator.

The opinions expressed are interesting, and the pictures so violate our sex-role expectations as to be an education in themselves. As a free-loan film, this work is definitely a worthwhile addition to the study of sexism, stereotypes, and career choices. It should work with almost any age and type of audience.

The film presents so many images and opinions in its 28 minutes that only by stopping the projector two or three times during its run can even a small portion be discussed—a major weakness. Schools are provided with nine spirit masters and a leader's guide to supplement the film, but I have not seen this support material.

Anything You Want to Be is an effort by AT&T to change its image and the court-backed opinion of many that Ma Bell is herself a sexist employer. It is good corporate public relations and good education.

28 minutes, color, directed by Susan Wayne (1976). Available free-of-charge on loan from some Bell Telephone Offices. Contact your local Bell Telephone Business Office.

Arthur and Lillie

This 1976 Academy Award nominee is an affectionate portrait of Arthur and Lillie Mayer. Arthur Mayer, now 89, worked as head publicist for Paramount Pictures promoting Mae West, operated the Rialto Theater in New York where he earned the nickname [the] "Merchant of Menace" for his policy of running monster films, distributed films to the Allied troops during World War II, and pioneered in

bringing to America foreign films such as *Open City* and *Bicycle Thief.* At age 70 he "retired" and was invited to speak to a university film class on the mistaken notion that he was really Louis B. Mayer of MGM fame.

The students liked him so much that he was invited back and today spends much of the year teaching in the film departments at Stanford, Dartmouth, and USC.

Lillie was one of the original suffragettes and lifelong helper of Arthur. Nearing 90, they travel together and form a community of students wherever they go. *Arthur and Lillie* is an engaging look at the early business of Hollywood, but it is also a portrait of graceful aging and *joie de vivre* at 90. The couple is presented not so much because of Arthur's reminiscences about the early motion picture industry but because they prove that age and joy can go together and that a marriage can do more than survive.

29 minutes, color, directed by Jon Else, Kristine Samuelson, and Steven Kovacs (1975). From Pyramid Films; rental also from Viewfinders or University of California.

At 99

The University of Maryland Center on Aging recently examined 549 children's books in a local county library system. Only 16 percent of them portrayed older people in the story, whereas less than 5 percent had pictures of older people. Perhaps most telling, the words "old," "little," and "ancient" accounted for 84 percent of all adjectives used to describe old people in the books studied.

"Children's books are perpetuating this ridiculous myth of the do-nothing, boring, invisible aged person," explains Dr. Edward Ansello, the study director. "Here's the first real learning experience about the aged, and kids don't learn about older people being interesting and important in their own right."

There are numerous new short films that attempt to undo this stereotype. One of the best is *At 99.* Ninety-nine happens to be the age of Louise Tandy Murch—vivacious, lively of intellect, and more supple of body than many people 50 years her junior. She believes in the power of positive thinking and serves as living proof of its validity. She talks at old folks homes and explains that many of the aged are depressed because they believe that "old" is no good. Her message is that you must "think positively, 'I'm not so bad after all.' "

Louise Murch is not simply young for her age; she's young period. At a mere 90 she began a yoga class and now does exercises that would put many high school students to shame—and this in spite of a pin in each hip. She frequents a health food store, avoids both white sugar and television as equally destructive, and still plays a lively piano.

At 99 is a film that helps destroy the stereotype of the aged as infirm, senile, and joyless. It should provoke those who view youth as holy and the inevitability of aging as an obscenity to question their views.

Filmmakers and distributors have recently been quite taken with films of the handicapped and aged who are exceptions. The much more difficult task of presenting a strong statement about a typical old person or cripple has yet to be accomplished. Perhaps some filmmaker will make the ultimate film about the 95-year-old-paraplegic who dances ballet and farms 100 acres. But until then, films such as *At 99* provide a healthy look at the potential of life after 90.

24 minutes, color, directed by Deepa Saltzman (1974). Rental from Viewfinders or University of California.

Automania 2000

"If people are to be brought together again, given a chance to get acquainted with each other and involved in nature, some fundamental solutions must be found to the problems posed by the automobile."

Edward T. Hall, The Hidden Dimension

In *The Secular City*, Harvey Cox pictured technopolitan man as a driver in a cloverleaf intersection. As such, he is mobile and has the freedom of choice. But what if the automobile, instead of freeing man, enslaves him. What if cars are produced to be *sold* rather than to be *used* so that their function as transportation is secondary to their function as a symbol of social standing, power, or ownership? Such are the questions explored in this Halas-Batchelor award winning film.

In the year 2000, man is pictured as the loser in his battle with the automobile. Self-reproducing cars are piled 17 deep, cars and houses are identical, and the city is totally immobilized while still more cars are produced. The satiric vision of *Automania 2000* has both humor and insight.

The film simply extends our current attitude toward the auto to its logical extreme and points out the need for social change. A discussion of the personal meaning of the automobile is inevitable after viewing the film. Other themes worth treating are the "more is better" attitude, the idea of "progress," the effects of affluence, and possible solutions to the auto epidemic. The film was an Academy Award nominee.

10 minutes, color (1964). From McGraw-Hill Films; rental also from Viewfinders.

Automatic

This Czechoslovakian animation is a simply drawn story of a man who works on an assembly line making slots in some sort of vending machine. When payday arrives, he goes to a coin machine just like the kind he makes and receives his pay. To spend his hard-earned money, he can buy food from other vending machines (that flash an automatic "thank you"), insert money in a love machine that returns hugs and kisses, or take advantage of a variety of other machines that sometimes work and sometimes dispense a glass of bolts instead of water.

Our innocent hero becomes the victim of a police search (the police emerge from the TV set), and much of the film is taken up with a good old cops-and-robbers chase sequence. He finally escapes and goes back to work. But before he can start, he opens his slot-like mouth and inserts a coin. The world is truly automatic.

About 10 minutes, color, animation. From Phoenix Films; rental also from Viewfinders.

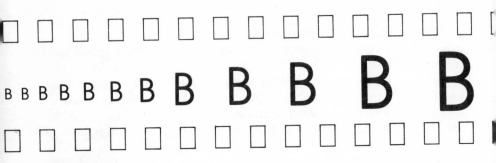

Baggage

Baggage is a subtle, lyrical, and totally visual film that uses the ancient art of mime to present an allegory about the burden of a heavy conscience.

Japanese mime Mamako Yoneyama carries an invisible piece of baggage that represents guilt. She first takes her burden to a confessional. But the priest is a mechanical functionary unable to offer either forgiveness or empathy.

Taking her burden outside, she finds a pond with ducks and swans. There she forgets her guilt, exalting in play and imitation of the birds. But the innocence of the birds is not hers, and the baggage once more imposes itself. She kicks and hits the burden but ultimately picks it up and walks along a beach.

At the seashore, she meets a Neptune-like figure who almost offers to take the load but instead leaves her standing alone. Next she enters an airport terminal and deposits the baggage in a locker, after which she enjoys a brief respite from guilt and finds freedom and joy. But reflections of herself in water and glass force a self-confrontation that refuses to permit her such an easy escape. And the baggage reappears.

At a playground, her burden is symbolically lightened as she watches children at play, but the spell is broken, and the baggage reassumes its awful weight. She approaches a series of strange seaside structures that look like mechanical giants from another planet. Nevertheless, they also are unable to bear the ever-increasing weight of the baggage.

Now, nearly broken, she returns to the airport terminal where the baggage counter and the flight of planes represent escape. She places the baggage on an airline scale and "falls dead." She has finally escaped the burden.

Baggage contains black and white cinematography as fine and delicate as that in any short film. It speaks in the language of elemental symbols—water, reflections, upward and downward movement, barriers and passageways, and light and dark. Using this symbolic language, the film weaves a psychomoral tale. Mamako is not so much a person as a conscience, a spiritual personality. The film does not end with a physical death; the shot of Mamako boarding the plane makes this clear.

The baggage represents guilt, a burden that increases in weight unless cleansed. Mamako is freed from the burden only in play and fantasy, such as when she identifies with the innocence of the birds and the children. Water is a source of ablution but also of reflections in which reality can be seen. The airport and its planes represent escape but also spiritual death.

The scenes of San Francisco act more as a character in the film than a mere backdrop, dramatizing Mamako's entrapment and powerlessness. She tries to give her burden to others—the priest, the sea god, the mechanical creatures, the airport locker—only to find that such a burden cannot be given away. Her "death" and parts of her journey are replete with Christian symbolism, offering yet another level of interpretation for the film.

Baggage is a cinematic poem that requires viewer effort to unravel. It is a film with many levels of meaning, yet with a striking surface grace and beauty. No one will understand everything in the film from a single viewing, but a group can share insights and explore its depths with rich rewards.

22 minutes, black and white, directed by Alexander Neel (1969). From Paramount; rental also from Viewfinders.

Banks and the Poor

This is one of the most instructive documentaries I have ever viewed. There have been thousands of films made about bank robbers, but *Banks and the Poor* is the only one in existence that shows how banks rob people. This NET film is advocate journalism at its best, carefully documenting how the poor and the middle class are victimized by banks and loan companies.

David Rockefeller, chairman of the board of Chase Manhattan Bank, claims that the banking profession has paid special attention to the disadvantaged. To refute his claims, the film examines the ties between banks and real estate firms and details how little capital has gone to finance low-income housing. Banks help finance slumlords but refuse loans to the poor. Those refused at "full-service banks" turn to finance companies such as Beneficial. A hidden camera at a loan company office is used to record an interview with a man who makes about $158 a week. He applies for an $800 loan, which is approved. His interest rate? Twenty-five and a half percent per year. And where does the finance company get the money to loan the man? From the same bank that turned him down. Is the risk of the poor defaulting so high as to justify the astronomical interest rate? Ninety-five percent of all borrowers, even the poor, pay back loans.

The film goes on to document more ways in which banks oppress and serve the status quo. For example, ghetto credit swindlers could be stopped by banks using their considerable financial clout.

Banks and the Poor manages to make a relatively static subject visually interesting without sacrificing thoroughness.

59 minutes, black and white. From University of California and Indiana University.

Bate's Car

If I were to say that *Bate's Car* is about a method of automobile propulsion involving methane, you might leave the film to the science department; but that would be your loss. Perhaps I had better say that the film is about the creative spirit, about the value of individual initiative in a world dominated by corporations, about alternate lifestyles, or even about ecology.

Harold Bate lives in rural southwest England and drives a car powered by pig manure—actually by the methane gas produced by a mixture of this manure with straw and lime. The gas is 127 octane, produces no carbon monoxide, and burns very cleanly. Fifty pounds of manure produces about three gallons of gas. The film shows Bate riding through the English countryside in his methane car and explaining its advantages. His explanation of how the manure is converted to methane and fed into the engine is a bit confusing (perhaps intentionally), but that matters little. Bate makes it all sound and look simple.

Bate has received 10,000 requests from all over the world, including inquiries from American companies that want to produce his engine. But Bate has little time for wheeling and dealing. At a ripe old age, the inventor is now at work on a self-propelled bicycle. Every time the rider goes over a bump, and therefore places weight on the saddle, the movement is transferred to the wheels. The rougher the road, the faster you go. Bate still has one bug to iron out on the bicycle—how to stop it.

An important message of *Bate's Car* is that an individual can retain his simplicity and do something significant without working for a big corporation or big money. The film could even be used in career education: Why always teach students that a "career" means working for someone else?

16 minutes, color. Produced by the National Film Board of Canada. From Arthur Mokin Productions; rental also from University of California.

Beauty Knows No Pain

One of the few differences between a Marine and a Kilgore Rangerette is that a Rangerette has to smile all the time. Both go through a rigorous boot camp and training. Both learn to function with machine-like precision as part of a team. Both are told that membership in the group will enhance their desirability and humanity. Both belong to a group that is carefully selected and where many desire membership but few are accepted. Both thrive on patriotism and engage in hazing newcomers. Both are viewed by some as heroes and embodiments of the American Dream, while others consider them outmoded and dangerous examples of the death of the American spirit.

Beauty Knows No Pain is a documentary about the training of Kilgore College Rangerettes. The Rangerettes are a group of pretty young girls who fulfill the fantasies of males during half time at football games and parades around the country. Their director is Gussie Nell Davis, a sometime sergeant, sometime Southern grandmother. She firmly believes that a Rangerette learns "to be a lovely poised young lady, dependable, able to live a morally sound life and have values that fit with society, yet be individuals."

The film's director, Elliott Erwitt, believes the whole operation to be a ridiculous travesty—a forced conformity for empty-headed females. He reveals his contempt for the group through his choice of camera angles, editing, and selection of images. The film ends with the posting of the final list of those girls (identified only by number) who have made the "team" for next year. The girls rush to the board and erupt into an orgy of emotion with everyone crying from either joy or anguish.

After the film, many students will agree with the director's point of view, but some girls will want application blanks for the Rangerettes. This varied reaction is what makes *Beauty Knows No Pain* an excellent discussion vehicle. The film was first shown on TV as part of NET's *Great American Dream Machine*. A teacher's guide is supplied, but it misses the point of the film.

25 minutes, color. From Benchmark Films; rental also from Viewfinders and University of California.

The Bet

Ron Waller is a professional filmmaker who made *The Bet* to show off his ability. His goal was "to do everything on this film that is possible for one person to do, without any help." He succeeded; he has made a gripping suspense film all by himself and won his private bet with those who said it couldn't be done.

Waller's virtuoso craftsmanship is evident throughout this story of a man who agrees to live utterly alone for five years to prove he can survive loneliness and isolation. The film bears the title and inspiration of an Anton Chekhov short story but captures none of the original's depth. *The Bet* resembles the original Chekhov as much as John Huston's *The Bible* resembles its inspiration. Chekhov wrote of capital punishment versus imprisonment, about freedom and truth; he created a work of art. *The Bet* is an exercise in cinematography, a finely crafted ego-trip.

For film study the work is excellent, especially in conjunction with Waller's feature article in the February 1969 issue of *American Cinematographer*. For literature study, however, stick to the printed original.

24 minutes, color. From Pyramid Films.

A Better Train of Thought

This Hungarian animation effort is a clever parable with multiple meanings. An old steam-powered train filled with passengers chugs along. The passengers are a happy bunch until a faster, more modern-looking train whizzes past. They then become impatient with their tired engineer and demand a new one who can catch the faster train. The new, apelike engineer shovels coal faster but to no avail. He too is kicked off, and the passengers demand another. This one bathes the train in grease, which succeeds only in producing much wheel spinning.

While the search for the perfect engineer continues, one pops up with plans for what looks like a new train—a turbo train. But he is rejected and finally leaves the train with the plans tucked under his arm.

More engineers try in vain to catch up. One uses the services of a caged bird. Another is a brutal dictator who demands that the passengers make sacrifices and eliminate excess baggage. Still another makes the passengers push. A scientifically minded engineer finally redesigns the old engine, and the train takes off in a burst of speed to the applause of the passengers. The successful engineer is given a medal, but the camera pulls back to reveal that the train is not traveling under its own power. A huge turbo train pushes it, then picks it off the tracks and tosses it aside like a pesky fly.

A Better Train of Thought (pardon the pedestrian title) is a parable with universal application. It fits very well as a description of our current energy crisis; it describes a nation in need of a revolution instead of a reformation; it is about any system (a school system, for example) that has outlived its usefulness and needs more than a new engineer. It is about the rejection of the prophet in his own country, and it describes various commonly proposed solutions to any crisis.

10 minutes, color, animated, written and directed by Attila Dargay (1974). From Stephen Bosustow Productions.

Betty Tells Her Story

This is an excellent film for generating discussion in a class or course about self-image or for women's groups exploring the nature of identity and social values.

Filmmaker Liane Brandon simply films Betty sitting and telling a story about buying a new dress. She tells of her purchase of a very expensive dress to wear at the Governor's Ball. Shortly after the purchase the dress is stolen. The story is the kind that might be told over coffee between two housewives, seemingly of little import. But for Betty the incident was far more complex. The filmmaker has Betty tell her story a second time.

In this second telling, Betty reveals her feelings about the incident. She tells how the dress made her feel pretty and admired for the first time in her life. Yet the admiration and praise from others made her uncomfortable since she knew that she was being complimented for a prettiness she didn't have. Her body language and voice in the second telling reveal how the incident is symptomatic of her current feelings about herself. "I had the feeling I had lost more than the dress. I knew I would never find it again."

Betty Tells Her Story is film-as-therapy for both Betty and any viewers who can identify with her. Women viewers are more likely to find the film an emotional experience than men even though Betty's experience is universal and not limited to women and pretty dresses.

20 minutes, black and white. From New Day Films; rental also from University of Michigan.

The Big Shave

The camera unflinchingly records a man shaving. He nicks himself once, finishes, but decides that the shave is not close enough. He shaves again and nicks himself again; a bit of blood flows. He continues shaving and cuts himself again and again on the face and throat until he is covered with blood from ears to chest.

More blood is shed in the six minutes of *The Big Shave* than in most violent feature films. Through all this butchery, the man remains calm, and at the film's end seems satisfied that his shave is now close enough.

The film—black humor of the goriest sort—will produce a strong audience reaction. It is valuable precisely because it produces such a reaction. Some viewers will think it disgusting; others will call it one of the funniest they've ever seen. After viewing, discuss the reasons for the different reactions among viewers.

6 minutes, color, directed by Martin Scorsese (1968). Rental from Viewfinders and University of California.

16 B

Bing, Bang, Boom

A few years ago Marshall McLuhan gained international fame by writing a book few people understood. He claimed that we are moving into an era of acoustic space, a time of trading in the eye for the ear. He also claimed that schools traditionally operate on a rearview mirror principle, constantly preparing students to live in the generation just past. Smart fellow, this McLuhan; too bad he never learned common-people English. If he is right that we are moving into the auditory era, he is also right about the schools. Schools are only now beginning to introduce courses in visual awareness; they have yet even to think of exploring acoustic space.

But back in 1969 the National Film Board of Canada made a film about R. Murray Schafer, an educator who does explore with students the world of sound. Most of the film shows Schafer working with a seventh-grade music class. He has students listen and "write down" every sound they hear; he has them draw a sound and determine its color. He leads them on an acoustic walk and questions what they hear, always refining their verbal ability to explore sound. He has them listen for silence (they conclude it is impossible), listen to heart beats, make sounds of their own—the softest and loudest, the most repulsive and most beautiful, the longest and shortest, the sounds of a cactus or a tree. Finally the students compose a "symphony" of their sounds, and the resultant cacophony resembles the cookie monster performing a work by John Cage.

Schafer's ideas are quite easily adaptable to any grade level—even college. The film is weak on explaining the philosophy of why sound requires sensitivity on the part of the listener. But for teachers who can see the value of exploring acoustic space, this film could give some new teaching ideas.

24 minutes, black and white (1969). From NFBC; rental also from University of California.

A Bird's Life

This Czechoslovakian animation is a genuinely funny film. *A Bird's Life* might be more than pure entertainment; it could be a cockeyed parable about women's liberation. Let the audience decide.

The main character is a woman who feels "tied down" by her overwhelming chores, overflowing pots, and overbearing family. She, along with her husband and son, attends a magic show at the local cabaret. The kid pushes his mom on stage, and she becomes a volunteer for a hypnotist, who tells her that she is really a bird.

Sure enough, she takes off, flies through an open window, and begins to enjoy her new-found freedom as a bird. Naturally, her family is upset and tries to get her back down to earth. Most of the film is devoted to the humorous efforts of family and society to end this flight from normality. The characters, drawn to resemble Charles Addams's cartoon figures, look comic, and that is half the battle in a humorous animation film.

The problem of the flying mother is finally solved with an ironic twist when the hypnotist is called back to work his magic on the father and son. Once he is finished, the family of three bird-people flap about contentedly and perhaps live happily ever after.

A Czechoslovakian animation that is hilarious is rare; any film that is both humorous and has a "message" is even rarer. *A Bird's Life* is both and well worth the price of admission.

9 minutes, color, animation. From Macmillan Films.

Blake

Who hasn't at some time admired the freedom of the wind or a bird, both unbound by cities, traffic lights, and the duties of earning a living? Everyone dreams of being "free as a bird," but Blake James has the courage to live a life that others only dare to dream.

Blake has a freedom machine—a yellow biplane small enough to be pushed around like a wheelbarrow and yet large enough to gain the freedom of the skies. Blake hates cities, lives in a cluttered log cabin in the country, and frequently takes off on cross-Canadian air trips that last as long as two years.

While on the ground, he drives a barely living Volkswagen that starts with a screwdriver. His economic philosophy simply stated is "What you don't spend, you don't have to earn." He earns what he must by working as an illustrator in a city office just long enough to finance his flights of fancy.

When the city becomes a prison and the sky turns blue with promises of unbridled escape, Blake returns to his cabin to prepare for another unhurried jaunt in the air. During the entire film, Blake never says a word. Instead, off-camera voices of people who know Blake talk about him as if he were a mythical hero. From the admiring voices we learn of the man Blake who excites others by his own sense of freedom, of the Blake who impresses young girls as sweet, innocent, and childlike, of the Blake who can't stand to be tied down with possessions and who loses himself in the sky without navigational aids, parachute, lights, or radio.

His preparations finally complete, Blake bounces his plane down the field that serves as his runway. He takes off, not to get anywhere, but simply to enjoy the experience of flying alone in an open cockpit. He cruises along happily, playing his harmonica and flirting with the birds who must consider him more one of their own than a human riding in a machine. When he nears Montreal, the polluted air and nearly empty gas tank force a landing. Blake calmly floats down into the Montreal airport, confounding the tower controllers who view him as "some kind of nut." His fur coat and nonchalant style contrast with the highly mechanized and efficient airport. Blake cuts a tiny figure in these massive surroundings, his yellow plane nearly laughable compared to the majestic jet liners. He seems to be from another age, as much a misfit in the airport as in the rest of the city.

Blake refuels and takes off again. His map blows out of the cockpit but the loss doesn't phase him; his whereabouts make little difference. When dusk forces him to land, he settles for the nearest treeless field, and goes to sleep under his plane.

When he awakes at dawn, a small boy greets him curiously and again we see the contrast between Blake and other ordinary humans of less than mythical proportions. The boy is equipped with space-age toys, his one-way astronaut helmet contrasting with Blake's goggles. The heroes the boy has been given to admire and imitate live in capsuled environments and work in teams. It is their world of modern technology that finds Blake a freak, but it is this same world that stands in awe of his sense of freedom.

The attitude of Blake the dreamer captures the spirit of a pioneer in early America or an explorer of the New World. He would have been at home several hundred years ago, or even as late as World War I, the era of all his flying heroes. But in the 1970s he is an oddity wherever he goes.

19 minutes, color, directed by Bill Mason (1969). From Pyramid Films; rental also from Viewfinders and University of Michigan.

Blaze Glory

Blaze Glory is a slapstick spoof on the traditional characters and plot of the cowboy movie. Sneering villains hold up a stage coach to start the rousing action. But nearby, taking a meticulous bath in a handy stream, is our indomitable hero—Blaze Glory. Unseen by them, Blaze slips into his spotless costume and pounces on the robbers. But curses! He is foiled when one of the dastardly thieves uses a damsel from the stagecoach to escape. The chase is on.

In the course of ten minutes, Blaze rescues the damsel (a number of times) and is ultimately victorious without suffering so much as a crease in his white trousers and chaps. Since horses are nonexistent in the film, its characters "ride" in the air thanks to an animation technique Norman McLaren (see *The Eye Hears, the Ear Sees*, p. 54) has called "pixilation." Blaze is covered with white powder, and the damsel blinks her eyelashes appropriately. The villains are dressed in

black, twirl their necessary mustaches, and sneer to frighten said damsel.

The film lacks the sharpness and subtlety of *A Special Report* but does take the clichés of a genre to their wildest extremes.

10 minutes, color, directed by Chuck Menville and Len Janson. From Pyramid Films; rental also from Viewfinders.

The Blessings of Love

This is a simple animated film filled with the power to evoke deep feelings. The story line is simply that of a boy who becomes a man, falls in love, marries, and in old age follows his wife in death. As a youth, the man fantasized a love for a beautiful woman. Later he finds the woman and marries her. In middle age he fantasizes his wife as a younger, sexier woman. Finally, after his wife's death, he imagines that she is still present.

"We all lead temporary lives," said Camus. And nowhere is this more evident than in an examination of a lifetime of fantasies. The youngster can hardly wait to become a teenager, the high school freshman dreams of himself as a big senior, while the seniors dream of college. As one fantasy is fulfilled, another takes its place until death ends all.

Older viewers will see much of themselves in the film and will feel that *The Blessings of Love* is both beautifully and tragically accurate. Younger viewers will also see the truth of the film but are more likely to offer varying opinions on what the film "means." The film is so simple in story line and technique yet so provocative of contrasting opinions and emotions that it is an excellent animation for showing to almost any group. More and more film users complain of the utter pessimism of animated films. Those who find this complaint valid will recognize *The Blessings of Love* as a refreshing change.

9 minutes, animated, color. From Macmillan Films.

BLT

This is a film designed to combat a malady that afflicts most Americans today—Eater's Alienation (EA). People suffering from EA have come to believe that only chemists know what is in all those meat packages so neatly arranged in supermarket rows and bathed in Muzak and fluorescent light all day. EA parents have only minor problems telling their children where babies come from, but few have mustered the courage to tell the truth about meat eating. Just try to tell some four-year-old that he's going to have a cow or a pig for supper.

BLT begins with some rather romantic footage of pigs in early morning sunlight—all of which proves that almost anything looks nice in dawn's ethereal haze. The notorious mud bath is presented not as something dirty or ugly but as a sensuous experience—as all children secretly know already. *BLT* filmmaker Art Ciocco might have vegetarian leanings. At least, he believes that pigs have received a bad press and is out to change their image. But these beautiful creatures, these cuddly and sensuous innocents, must serve man—so it's off to the slaughterhouse. If the camera were to continue inside the slaughterhouse, a few converts to vegetarianism might be won. After all, vegetables don't scream out loud. But the doors remain mercifully shut, and the viewer is asked to use his imagination. For a final shot, the film moves to a restaurant where a patron calmly orders a bacon, lettuce, and tomato sandwich (a "BLT" in restaurant jargon).

BLT is a nice film for children and also a philosophical reminder that we are merely other creatures rearranged and that life goes on only through the mutual slaughter and ingestion of various species.

14 minutes, color. From Paramount Films.

The Boarded Window

The Boarded Window has been well received by reviewers and film festival judges. It won a CINE Golden Eagle and a Bronze Medal at the Chicago International Film Festival. Indeed, the film is exceptionally well made for a low-budget student production. In spite of its merits, however, the film raises a question in regard to good taste and possibly even obscenity.

The Boarded Window is a film adaptation of Ambrose Bierce's short story of the same title. The film begins with the burial of its main character, an old fur trapper who lived alone for many years in his log cabin in the wilderness. There is a mystery about this man; his cabin has but one window, and that has been boarded up for years. No one knows why. By means of a film-length flashback, we discover the chilling secret.

The young trapper is out checking his traps and finds them all sprung, the bait missing, but no animal captured. Strange rustlings in the woods add to the building suspense and feeling of terror. He returns at nightfall to his cabin with its single opening, a hole in the wall unprotected by glass or shutters. His wife is taken with a severe fever and dies in the morning. He lovingly prepares her for burial and maintains vigil by her side all day. His vigil continues into the night and he falls asleep sitting next to the corpse. Suddenly there is a noise, viewers' hearts beat faster, and the suspense becomes nearly unbearable. Something else is in the cabin. A shotgun blast shatters the quiet, and in its light we see the head of a mountain lion. We are so pulled into the film that even the obviously stuffed animal elicits gasps and shrieks from the audience.

Morning arrives, and the camera pans with excruciating slowness around the cabin to reveal the terror behind the mystery of the boarded window. The dead wife had been attacked by the mountain lion, which entered through the open window. The camera reveals the gory, blood-covered corpse with the remains of a paw stuck in its mouth. From that day on, the window was boarded.

The Boarded Window is a successful film judged on technical merit and on its ability to involve an audience. My only argument with it concerns its explicit depiction of gore. Could not the terror be culminated without the cheap trick of plastic wounds and simulated blood? Viewers of horror films expect to be shocked, and they watch because they want their emotions violently manipulated. But I feel as if I had gone along with the storyteller and allowed him to lead my emotions only to be rewarded by a pail of blood thrown in my face.

Of course, students raised on stories of body snatchers and teenage cannibals might not find the film quite so offensive. Perhaps it should be shown just to raise the issue of the explicit depiction of violence.

17 minutes, color, directed by Alan Beattie (1974). From Perspective Films; rental also from Viewfinders and University of California.

The Boy Who Liked Deer

This film from LCA is part of the same "Learning to Be Human" series that includes *Shopping Bag Lady*. Jason is a junior high student who is a "nice boy" but seems to have little to do except let air out of tires in parking lots and phone in false alarms. His home life is minimal, and his one love seems to be the deer at the local deer park where he helps the warden at feeding time. He looks forward to the summer when he can work at the park as a volunteer.

At school Jason is, to say the least, unenthused. In Mr. Mason's English class he fails to do his assignment and almost falls asleep when the teacher begins reading from his autographed first edition of E.E. Cumming's poetry. Later Mason informs Jason that he will need to attend summer school. Infuriated that he will not be able to work at the deer park, Jason and his friends break into school for a vandalism spree. Immediately after Jason has destroyed Mr. Mason's first edition, the teacher returns to the classroom and Jason hides. He sees the pain in Mr. Mason's eyes as he sees the destruction and hears him weep over the loss of his beloved book. Jason begins to realize the meaning of loss and hurt, but the real impact remains for later.

Jason and his friends next climb a fence into the deer park to frighten the animals. Jason protests but goes along and joins them in ripping open feed bags; but none of the boys notices that rat poison is being mixed with the feed in the process. The next day the warden asks Jason's help in carting off some of the dead deer. Jason has not been caught by the "authorities," but he cannot escape his own self-recrimination. At last he knows what it means to suffer loss.

The Boy Who Liked Deer is well scripted and realistically acted. The plot is quite believable and should be useful for a discussion of vandalism, anger and its displacement, boredom, loss, and the communication of emotions.

18 minutes, color, written by Dinitia McCarthy and directed by Barbara Loden (1975). From LCA; rental also from MMM.

Broken Treaty at Battle Mountain

Robert Redford narrates this sensitive and compassionate documentary on the struggle of the Shoshone Indians to regain 24 million acres of Nevada that they lost in their 1863 treaty with the Federal government. Many of the recent "pro-Indian" films are so general in their approach that they fail to move the viewer to anything more than a vague feeling of injustice. The specificity of *Broken Treaty at Battle Mountain* is its strength, yet it uses this one legal battle as the basis for studying the more universal issue of the destruction of a culture and the ultimate death of the Indians as a people.

The government contends that the Battle Mountain Treaty was a bum deal for the Indians but, nevertheless, a valid treaty. The traditional members of the Shoshone Tribes contend that the treaty leaves the land in their hands, and they have considerable legal opinion on their side. The government has offered $1.05 an acre as a "goodwill gesture," but the traditionals have refused the offer, since acceptance of payment would jeopardize their claims to ownership.

The government has forbidden the Indians to hunt for food on "their own" land while allowing white hunters to hunt for sport, leaving piles of deer carcasses behind to rot. The government is also in the process of destroying the pinyon trees on "Indian land" to make more room for the white cattle raisers despite the fact that the Indians use the tree for food and consider it sacred. The "chain dragging" of the pinyon groves with a huge chain tied to two bulldozers climaxes the film and summarizes the attack on Indian life and culture by the machines and life-style of the surrounding white society.

Redford narrates the film in an understated manner; the editing and camera work are excellent. Director Joel Freedman spent two years making *Broken Treaty at Battle Mountain*, and his care shows. Stanley Kauffman called this film "better than any documentary I've seen on the subject."

60 minutes, color (1975). From Soho Cinema.

Burlington Diner

Is Harry Bouras a mad man as he wanders about in a dining car restaurant claiming that in its artifacts one can see the whole history of American art? Is *Burlington Diner* just a put-on good for a few laughs, or is it an amazing statement on the relation between art and reality? An audience of hundreds of media teachers laughed almost constantly during most of the film when I first saw it, but I remained in silent awe at mad Harry's ability to see meaning where others saw merely utilitarian objects. Both responses are probably "valid," and both make *Burlington Diner* worth viewing, especially in units on creativity, perception, art, or pop culture.

24 B

Bouras sees a row of water glasses as a Duchamp-like dada sculpture; the cook with his flapjacks is a potential George Segal sculpture; the diner itself is an Edward Hopper painting come to life. Even the congealed paint on a NO PARKING sign reveals itself as art, and the drippings from workmen become an illustration of art-as-process. Pop, op, neon, garbage can, neo-real, funk, New York school—they're all in the diner for those with eyes and the audacity to look.

20 minutes, color. From Vision Quest.

But First This Message

This film, produced by Action for Children's Television in 1971, has since been used by countless groups to encourage discussion about the effects of TV on kids. In its brief 15 minutes it can only hint at some of the possible influences. The film points out that kids watch more TV before they enter school than college students spend in obtaining a degree. Television has confirmed Freud's statement (or warning) that "if you give a child to me for the first six years he will be mine forever after." The confirmation has not come from psychiatrists but from A.C. Nielsen researchers.

The film's strongest impact is generated by showing the faces of children watching TV. Those who see TV as evil can read much into those blank faces. Excerpts from commercials shown on just one hour of Saturday kidvid on just one station reveal how regularly kids are subject to oversell for toys, cereal, and candy.

There is little new in *But First This Message*, nor is it a particularly well-made film. It has proven successful in generating discussion more because television is easy to talk about than because the film itself is a superior teaching device. *Television: The Anonymous Teacher* (see review in this book) is a more up-to-date and a more information-filled film than *But First This Message*. Both films are very similar in content, and both can be successfully used in units on the study of television and children. The weaknesses of *But First This Message* do not keep it from being useful.

15 minutes, color, directed by Yale Marc (1971). From ACT.

Buy, Buy

Buy, Buy features interviews with directors of TV commercials and shows bits of the filming of a cosmetic ad and one for Phillips Milk of Magnesia, the latter taking place in "Laxativeland."

The central fact of advertising, according to one director, is: "We're professionals and the consumer is an amateur. The best commercials are the ones you walk away from but they later come back to you."

Buy, Buy gives three specific examples of advertising techniques. A director notes that wide-angle lenses make "images explode . . . so a Capri can look like a Ferrari." In the Phillips commercial, the announcer is told to wear glasses to give him more authority. Another director explains that those ads which show tires running over glass and nails and sharp objects are a simple matter of editing—the parts where the tires failed are omitted, thus giving the impression of tire invulnerability.

Buy, Buy is the only film that voices the often-heard view of ad people that commercials are severely limited in their power to persuade. One director admits that "they can make people more aware and that's about it."

Buy, Buy leaves unanswered questions for discussion and room for divergent opinions. It also delves into the values of ads and their makers. Some of the interviews are weak in interest and repetitive, but in spite of these flaws, *Buy, Buy* ranks as the most honest film available about TV commercials.

20 minutes, color, directed by Donald MacDonald (who also did The Season). *From Churchill Films; rental also from University of Michigan.*

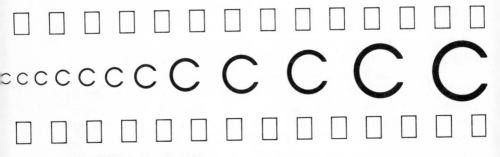

California Reich

The American Nazi Party (now calling itself the "National Socialist White People's Party") is alive, sick-as-ever, and might be living next door. This is the message of an Academy Award nominee for best documentary called *California Reich.* Filmmakers Walter Parkes and Keith Critchlow spent months getting acquainted with members of the California Nazi Party and winning their trust by explaining that they wanted only to make an honest, unbiased film. They succeeded well enough to shoot some truly remarkable footage of a group of everyday Nazis.

All the brown-shirted members wear the swastika arm band and consider the insignia a "symbol of your race." The party claims 2000 members who consider themselves (according to a recorded phone announcement) "an organization of decent, law-abiding white folks—just like you." They have meetings that resemble boy scout gatherings with the exception of the content of speeches, the ever-present swastika, and the nearly sacred picture of Adolf Hitler. They live in middle-class, split-level homes and hold respectable positions in local communities. Many are "closet Nazis," and few of their fellow workers would suspect that they go home to don swastika arm bands and brown shirts.

Since most viewers of the film are filled with horror and disgust at the sight of a swastika or a picture of Hitler, the act of watching "otherwise normal" people saluting Hitler or talking about the power of the swastika to "turn people to putty" is difficult to accept emotionally. Many viewers find the film almost black humor and laugh frequently during the documentary—partly from the incongruity of what appears and partly as a defense mechanism. How else can one react to a housewife who gives her favorite cake recipe and demonstrates how to decorate a cake with a swastika, using melted licorice in a field of white frosting? Or how should a viewer respond to a

C 27

five-year-old who proudly demonstrates his newly learned karate skills to use on "Jews and niggers"? And what emotions are appropriate as a group of well-scrubbed youths stand and pledge allegiance to "the immortal leader of my race, to the vision for which he stands, the hope and future of Aryan man"?

The central figure in *California Reich* is Allen Vincent, head of the San Francisco branch of the party. He spent 20 years in California prisons until finding a kind of salvation in the Nazi party. He calls himself a "victim of loneliness," and the filmmakers found that many Nazi members belong to the group because it strengthens weak egos.

A printed crawl at the end of the film reminds viewers that Hitler himself started with only a small group of men, and that "it could happen again." Many viewers, however, find the film more about a bunch of California kooks than about a threat to the United States.

Parts of *California Reich* were shown on television as part of *60 Minutes*, and the entire film might be shown later this year on PBS. A five-page article about the making of the film appeared in the November 1976 issue of *Filmmakers Newsletter*.

60 minutes, color, made in 1975—76 by Walter Parkes, Keith Critchlow, and others. From RBC.

Captain Mom

Captain Mom is a red-, white-, and blue-blooded American hero who awakens every morning to the stirring sounds of "The Star Spangled Banner" on his clock radio. After feeding his stuffed eagle and unlocking the five locks on his apartment, Captain Mom goes out into the world to live out the Boy Scout Oath, protect thankless little old ladies, and ogle the passing broads.

But this cross between Superman and the George Washington of fifth-grade history texts has a problem—he is unloved. So he seeks out love as he has seen others do, but meets only rejection. In desperation, he tries Compute-a-Date. Thanks to this American marvel of computer technology, he meets an arm-wrestling dreamboat. Saddened by his eventual defeat at the hands of the female Hercules, he attempts suicide. But, of course, such a hero is immune to knives and pills and leaps, even from the third story. Captain Mom is rescued from his emotional crisis, and the film has (sniff, sniff) a happy ending.

Captain Mom is a cleverly made film that mixes slapstick, caricature, and satire.

14 minutes, color, directed by Chuck Menville and Len Janson, who also did Blaze Glory *and* Vicious Cycles. *From CFS; rental also from Viewfinders.*

The Cave

The Cave is an animated version of the allegory of the cave in Book VII of Plato's *Republic*. To refresh your memory, the parable presents four prisoners chained together in an underground cave since childhood. They face a wall filled with moving shadows. One of the prisoners is released and realizes that these shadows, which he previously took for reality, are only imitations of a far greater reality. He returns to share his discovery with the other prisoners only to be rejected as a heretic. But the newly enlightened man makes it his task to share his knowledge with others. *The Cave* is a parable of illusion and reality, of mind-set and prejudice, of the power of knowledge and levels of awareness.

In addition to these traditional meanings, Plato's allegory takes on a new dimension in a society that experiences many of its emotions in a darkened movie house or in the projections from a television tube. The audience viewing the film version of *The Cave* is placed in a position much like Plato's prisoners, for it too is watching shadows that flicker across a screen.

Plato's cave can be considered the Bijou of the world. There is evidence to suggest that we, just like the prisoners, are slowly losing some of our ability to distinguish the real from the unreal because of all the time we spend watching life at second hand. We have all had, from such viewings, experiences so intense that they have become part of our memory banks and emotional psycho-history. We can easily separate a "real" memory from a memory of an image; we would never confuse a travelogue about Japan, for example, with an actual trip there. But when emotions enter the picture, no such easy distinction is possible. For the shocks, tears, fright, concern, joy, sorrow, and horrors we have felt in movie houses or on video are as real as those we experience elsewhere. The nervous system cannot tell the difference; the chemical reactions are identical. Therefore, deaths and battles, kisses and rebukes, all the stimulations we have received in movie houses or in front of our TV sets have played a large factor in our emotional education. And what these shadowy images have taught us is our ability, unprecedented in human history, to respond to the unreal as though it were real.

The images presented to us on screens are designed to manipulate our emotions. In real life we might not be able to distinguish clearly a threat from help, good from evil, or even love from hate. In films, complex "realities" are so unambiguously drawn that emotional confusion is absent. We may come to expect reality to be as clear as it is in the movies, and when it isn't, we may get confused and sometimes even emotionally handicapped. This is the all too common result of slick realities spoken in the language of Hollywood films.

Exactly how this conditioning has influenced us we don't know, for we are all still living in the cave of the electronic image. We have yet to find an escapee to report back to us on what life would be like without film and television, on how we would be emotionally different without this vast storehouse of pseudo-memories.

Plato's cave has a special meaning for us, and this animated version of it is a useful tool for exploring either the more traditional philosophical implications of the allegory or its meaning in an electronic shadow age.

10 minutes, color, narrated by Orson Welles. From Counterpoint Films.

The Cemetery of the Elephants

The Cemetery of the Elephants deserves to become a widely discussed film classic. It takes two moments from a lifetime, disregards the 40 years or so that separate them, and shows that a life can be defined by two such points.

In one moment, a boy prepares to leave his comfortable home and enter the inviting outside world. But before running into that world (he is not running "away") he eats, leaves a note for his still sleeping father, and types the title page for a story called "El Cementerio de los Elefantes." He locks the old black Corona portable typewriter and places it carefully in a compartment hidden under a floor tile.

The second moment is interwoven with the scenes of the boy's departure. An old man moves toward the house. First he emerges from a dark tunnel amid an eerie howling sound and proceeds through landscapes both desolate and stunningly beautiful. He approaches the house as the boy leaves; they pass within a few feet of each other but give no sign of recognition. They cannot speak across the few feet of space, for that space represents the distance of a single lifetime—the man and the boy are the same person.

The house the man enters is the same the boy left, but 40 years have passed and its sunny comfort has been blotted out by abandonment and neglect. He looks around, finds the hidden compartment, inserts the key, and removes the typewriter with the care of a priest removing a sacred object from the tabernacle—for this is his life. He sits down and begins to type; he has returned to the "Cemetery of the Elephants."

The film is a striking illustration of how cinematic time can be more revealing and profound than real time. In the course of only 17 minutes, viewers understand what "a lifetime" means. They see their own dreams and visions still being formed or older hopes gone unrealized.

Cemetery of the Elephants is an excellent film for film study, but it needs to be seen twice. Director Armando Robles Godoy (best known for his feature film, *The Green Wall*) upsets viewer expectations by planting a sense of impending shock that is never realized. Audiences tend to expect the young boy to shoot his father or the old man to discover a skeleton in the abandoned house. This false sense of doom misleads many viewers, especially those who fail to comprehend the oneness of the boy and man.

17 minutes, color, directed by Armando Robles Godoy (1975). From Films Inc.; rental also from Viewfinders.

Centers of Influence

The list of the 100 biggest-spending advertisers in 1974 featured the usual names in the top ten—Proctor and Gamble, GM, Sears, General Foods, etc. But there is one new, and some would say ominous, addition. The U.S. Government is now number 10, right behind Colgate-Palmolive, with ad expenditures of nearly 111 million dollars, mostly for military recruiting. Now that the draft has ended, the armed forces have discovered ad agencies and psycho-sell.

Centers of Influence is an informal film study of how the "new Army" sells young men on voluntary enlistment. Recruiters fresh from learning "dynamic selling" at the sales motivation institute show tanks and machine guns to wide-eyed high school boys. They plug the "new" army where rock concerts, underground papers, and discotheques seem to have replaced reveille and KP.

Excerpts from ads and recruiting films reveal that the comparison of the army to a glamorous sports team is common. One series of ads describes the "delayed entry program" as the greatest aid to a young male's love life since the uniform.

The film focuses on a recruiter in Hudson, New York, who believes that all the ads have produced "zilch so far." His approach is to help coach the high school football team and convince some of the players that the army could do wonders for their self-image. Running through the film is the theme of declining enlistments and the failure of recruitment efforts. But since *Centers of Influence* was made, the 111 million dollars has evidently paid off and recruiters are far more successful.

Centers of Influence is an excellent film to show to a group of high school students who might give army ads more than a passing glance. It could prevent some young men from being wooed into the army for the wrong reasons.

29 minutes, color. From the filmmaker, Ralph Arlyck Films.

Chickamauga

This is a film by Robert Enrico, who also made the famous *Occurrence at Owl Creek Bridge*. Taking an Ambrose Bierce short story as Alan

Beattie did in *The Boarded Window*, he creates a powerful drama of the innocence of childhood in confrontation with the horrors of war.

A seven-year-old deaf-mute living at the time of the Civil War wanders outside his yard to play. With his wooden sword, he battles a forest filled with imaginary enemies, all a microcosm of the very real war raging nearby. He falls asleep and awakens to head home, only to discover that he is in the middle of the retreating Union Army after the Battle of Chickamauga, one of the bloodiest in the Civil War.

But the boy accepts this pitiful scene as part of his fantasy, and so happily walks on the stomach of one dying man, rides the back of another, beats the drum still held by the dead drummer. A crawling man becomes a circus bear, the army tiny beetles, and himself the leader of a real army. Still unable to distinguish between fantasy and reality, he waves goodbye to his "playmates" and crosses the bloody stream to his home, now overrun by the army and in flames.

Familiar objects are burning and confuse him. He discovers his dead mother staring at him with unblinking eyes. He walks through the flames, throws his sword into the fire, and stares. He is still unable to comprehend what has happened; but who can? His deafness has already cut him off from much of reality, and now war makes his isolation complete.

The film is a powerful and moving experience (although many viewers will be unaware that the boy is deaf, since the film carries no narration or explanation). The film has many discussion angles, including the effect of war on future generations, the contrast between the bloody soldiers and the playful boy, and the inability of children to separate reality from fantasy.

33 minutes, black and white, directed by Robert Enrico (1963). From McGraw-Hill Films; rental also from Viewfinders, University of California, University of Michigan.

Children in Trouble: Alternatives to a National Scandal

This free-loan documentary is a superb example of persuasive filmmaking as well as an excellent treatment of the problem of juveniles and the law. The film powerfully documents the existing scandalous situation and proposes practical and effective alternatives to the problem.

Of the 8,000 persons sent each day to jails and penal institutions for the first time, 7,000 are children under 17 years of age. Of these thousands only one-third have committed a crime for which an adult would be incarcerated. Many have run away from school or home, and many are locked up because they have been abused, neglected, or even raped.

Children in Trouble (based on the book of the same title by Howard James) is a visually strong film that allows kids in jail to speak for themselves. The camera also moves candidly about places hypocritically named "correctional institutions" and allows the very walls and buildings to speak. A girl explains how it feels to be placed in a so-called "meditation room" as punishment; and boys are shown confined in what amounts to cages worse than those provided for zoo animals. A work gang of kids under the dictatorial direction of a guard are shown moving piles of coal as part of their vocational rehabilitation. In spite of failure rates as high as 90 percent and the fact that 75 percent of all adult criminals were once inside juvenile prisons, the system continues.

Having unquestionably documented the futility of the juvenile prison system, the film enters into a description of workable alternatives. In a brief ten minutes, it explains the operation of neighborhood homes with house parents, halfway houses and group homes, in-school suspension with special volunteer tutors, and community action programs, again utilizing volunteers.

The film is available free on a one-time basis for one to three consecutive days anywhere in the U.S. Donations are appreciated.

29 minutes, color, produced by The Film-Makers, Inc. (1974). Contact Children in Trouble Project, John Howard Association.

Cipher in the Snow

Cliff was a quiet boy, the sort no one noticed. His school record showed that he attended but was otherwise a real zero—a cipher.

One day while riding on the school bus, Cliff asks to be let out, walks to a snowbank, and dies. At school, the principal looks up Cliff's record and finds the teacher the boy had rated as "my favorite." The teacher says "I think he was in my math class last year" and is given the job of breaking the tragic news to the parents. No one admits to knowing Cliff; there is hardly enough information for a small obituary in the school paper.

Through flashbacks we see that Cliff had been neglected by his father, stepparents, and school. He caused no trouble and thus received no special attention. In the third grade he was described as a "slow learner," and he lived up to this expectation. When the coroner can find no obvious cause of death, the teachers examine themselves to find out why Cliff was such a stranger. One teacher concludes, "I think Cliff was erased away little by little until he finally went away." The teachers berate themselves for never having made Cliff feel like a human being.

The story effectively uses snow as a symbolic statement of the theme. Snowflakes, like people, are all unique yet look alike to a casual observer. The tragedy of neglect is like an avalanche; no individual snowflake admits responsibility. A good companion film is *Silent Snow, Secret Snow*, which uses some of the same symbolism to explore psychological death.

Cipher in the Snow is based on a short story by Jean Mizer that won an NEA-sponsored writing contest in 1964. It could be dismissed as a tear-jerker, but its message is certainly valid, if overstated. Production values are adequate, with an overall tone and style not unlike Sunday morning TV morality drama. The film could be used for a study of the need for acceptance and love, of teacher responsibility, or of the role of the school as a substitute parent.

24 minutes, color (1973). From Brigham Young University, Department of Motion Picture Production; rental also from University of California.

A Circle in the Fire

As little Virginia Cope tells her diary, "Three creepy boys came here today from out of nowhere." The three boys have arrived at her mother's dairy farm to admire the horses; they are greeted by her suspicion coated with only a thin veneer of friendliness. She is the kind of person so filled with fears and suspicions that they are bound to come true. As the film begins, Virginia tells her mother that the setting sun looks like fire, and her mother retorts, "You know how scared I am of fire on this place."

From that remark on, a feeling of impending disaster is maintained well by the filmmaker. The intimation of violence very near the surface of all the characters is sustained, flawed only by a few too many threatening sound effects and pregnant pauses.

The three boys, one of whom is related to a former worker on the farm, camp in the pasture and harass the Copes by letting out a bull, throwing stones at the mailbox, and riding the horses. As the housekeeper laments, "There ain't a thing you can do about it." After a threat to call the police, however, the boys pretend to leave. But as Virginia goes out to play, she discovers them horsing around in a watering tank. The boys admire the peace and beauty of the farm but seem intent on destroying what they can't have.

One boy claims, "If I had the chance, I'd build a big parking lot on it—or somethin." Instead, they set fire to the woods. The mother's worst fears are thus realized, and she helplessly watches the flames, dependent for her rescue on a few farm hands.

A Circle in the Fire is not an easy film to either discuss or understand. Victor Nunez has done a fine job of directing a difficult story. The acting is excellent, although the southern dialect is hard to follow early in the film.

50 minutes, color (1975). From Perspective Films; rental also from Viewfinders.

The City and the Self

This documentary is based on the ideas of Stanley Milgram and his research on the psychology of living in large cities. There are few, if any, nonfiction films about cities that offer as much food for thought and ideas per minute as *The City and the Self*.

This review is longer than most in order to make clear that Milgram's film has a relevance far beyond courses in urban studies. Psychology, language arts, communications, and social studies teachers would do well to consider showing *The City and the Self*.

The film begins by placing the viewer in a meditative mood for an early morning subway ride. The riders seem so far apart, so isolated. Those people off to one side, are they dozing or dying? What is the magic of those large sheets of paper held like a mask in front of so many faces? Is this some sunrise ritual? All those ads in the subway and outside, are they instructions from the government and how many thousands of them are there? Why is everyone hurrying, and why do they all look so grim? Suddenly, this meditation is rudely interrupted, as are so many processes in the city. A variety of people now give their opinions of living in New York: "Only in New York can you be three seconds late"; "It's a paranoid city"; "People are like bank vaults."

Stanley Milgram has some ideas about large cities, too, but his are based on experiments and research. He has found big city life to be governed by a series of exigencies caused by too many people living in too small a space. Human adaptations to such conditions are two-edged swords that contribute to survival yet produce much of what we feel is wrong with large cities.

Overload: Milgram stands on Fifth Avenue and explains that there is so much going on in a city that its inhabitants become very selective. This selectivity often appears as rudeness or coldness. His comments are quite hard to follow because of all the activity around him, thereby perfectly demonstrating the effects of overload.

Time: Since time is so precious, we have little to spare for the chance encounter. Meet one person and we give him an hour; meet a million people and we have time for no one.

Filters and boundaries: Cities are noted for limited access areas, doormen, an emphasis on privacy (or is it isolation?). There may be little contact with others in the marketplace; self-service is a convenience but also a way to eliminate human contact.

Institutions: Milgram stands on a littered sidewalk and asks passers-by why they don't pick up the trash. They explain, "It's not my job." In the city there are specialists for fires, crime, sickness, and so forth—even trash. And so we leave problems to the specialists and feel no responsibility. We need these men in uniforms, yet they simultaneously protect and estrange us from the environment.

Anonymity: Walk 150 feet from your house in the city and you're a total stranger. Milgram's experimenters make a large poster of a man who passes the same corner twice a day. They stand on the corner and offer $10 to anyone who can identify the face on the poster. No one can. In a small town where everyone knows everyone, there is a security that can be stifling. In the city where everyone is a stranger, there is a freedom that can be isolating.

Trust: Can we trust one another if we don't know one another? Experimenters knock on doors and ask, "Can I use your phone to call a friend whose house I can't find?" In small towns, 75 percent of the people help and let the stranger in; in the city, only 25 percent agree to help. Another experiment demonstrates that people will help others more when they are alone than when they are part of a crowd. Still another experiment shows that people who are bystanders to a set-up theft will neither stop the thievery nor report it.

But all is not alienation and mistrust in the city. There are wonderful surprises there and more variety and life than anywhere else in the world. And if man-as-crowd-member is unresponsive, man-as-individual will often as not help. Milgram's experiments found that asking for people's subway seats resulted in a 50-percent success rate. In disasters, fires, and floods, community feelings quickly develop. But the question is, how can we come closer without the fire, the flood, and the storm?

The City and the Self is well-filmed and edited. Harry From's direction keeps the action moving, and Milgram's narration is both well-written and well-delivered.

52 minutes, color (1974). From Time-Life Films.

Clever Village

This film is based on an old parable often recited in a multitude of tongues. Its origins are lost in time, but its meanings are timeless. A village is infested by a plague of snakes. One ingenious peasant proposes bringing in hedgehogs to devour the snakes; his solution is tried and it works. But now the hedgehogs become a problem, and foxes are called in to get rid of the hogs. Of course, after the foxes take over, hunters have to be called upon to rid the village of the foxes. This continues through a few more "solutions" until the village is ultimately destroyed.

The parable is a nice satire on the human tendency to "solve" problems by creating new ones. In economics, in the social sciences, and in lawmaking, one expects that solution A will lead to result B. Often the result is Y instead. On the other hand, if the solution has merit, "B" does indeed result, but invariably so do C, D, and E. If they didn't, what would all our legislators, police, psychiatrists, and social scientists have to do?

The "lessons" of the Clever-Village Syndrome can be applied to problem-solving in school affairs, local politics, and the national bureaucracy. A discussion of the film should be sure to deal with specific examples. For instance, the need for cheap labor in cities was "solved" by an influx of poor people; the presence of such "undesirables" led the more prosperous to flee the city for the suburbs, leaving slums behind in their flight; the slum problem was "solved" by building high-rise projects; the high-rise projects turned into concrete jungles. Anyone for foxes?

Discussion could also distinguish between "do-gooders" and "feel-gooders." A "do-gooder" is someone who *does* good. A "feel-gooder" is someone whose main concern is not helping others but being on the morally right side, which makes him feel righteous. "Feel-gooders" rarely take time to envision the consequences of their good acts. Bring on the hunters.

10 minutes, animated by Donyo Donev in Bulgaria. From McGraw-Hill Films.

Cold Rodders

If Pyramid Films were to release a film about snowmobiling, it would feature much slow motion and eloquent narration about the joys of hitting the drifts. Contemporary Films would find a snowmobile film made in Czechoslovakia complete with English subtitles. The Mass Media Ministries version would feature the snowmobile rider as symbolic of Christ's second coming. Half a dozen other distributors, mercifully unnamed here, would issue a film guaranteed to produce instant snores in all but the most fanatic collector of snowmobilia. But what about the National Film Board of Canada? One never knows what to expect from them, and that's why I watched *Cold Rodders* and was amply rewarded.

Cold Rodders is a devastating satire on the cult of the snowmobile. It begins innocently enough with shots of riders but soon gets down to business with film clips from TV ads for the machines. Next we join a family entering a snowmobile store to be outfitted with all the accessories including the proper clothing, follow a snowmobile race on a circular track, and ride along in a chauffeur-driven limousine that deposits one enthusiast at a resort dedicated to the pursuit of the joys of s.m. And, of course, there are many scenes of hordes of the yellow machines and bundled drivers invading the otherwise peaceful countryside.

The most devasting scene is a Catholic Mass said in an open field for a throng of snowmobilers and their machines. In the sermon, the priest reminds the cold rodders that they bear witness to man's need to get away from the city, to experience a reunion with God's nature. After Mass, the riders roar away to enjoy the "peace of nature" with enough noise to make the Indianapolis 500 sound like a hospital zone.

The theme of man-and-machine invading the unspoiled wilderness is a well-established tradition in American literature as well as life. Today that tradition is carried on by the "pioneers" who are the first in their neighborhood to buy a motorcycle, recreational vehicle, motorboat, jeep, camper, snowmobile, and who knows what next. *Cold Rodders* is fun to watch (unless you're an enthusiast yourself) and excellent for a study of satire, point of view, and the man/machine/nature conflict.

16 minutes, color. From NFBC; rental also from University of California.

The Collector

The Collector is a striking Zagreb animated metaphor. The classic man-versus-nature conflict is resolved with the tables turned on man. An obviously rich, colorfully dressed young man dreams of catching butterflies and goes out to fulfill his fantasy. After chasing the pastel creatures for a while, he falls exhausted. Along comes a huge and brightly colored butterfly, which hovers over the body, picks it up, and impales it on a large pin hanging on a wall where hundreds of other human trophies hang suspended. *The Collector* is a brilliant six-minute horror film with philosophic overtones.

6 minutes, color, animated, directed by Milak Blazekovic (1971). From Films Inc.; rental also from Viewfinders and University of Michigan.

Comforts of Home

This is a strange film, as befits an interpretation of a Flannery O'Connor short story. It manages to snowball comical elements into an avalanche of tragedy. An exasperating widow and her high school teacher son, Thomas, live together in a small Southern town. One day she takes in a delinquent girl in a well-intentioned effort at rehabilitation. Although the girl, Star, is nineteen and seemingly without morals, the widow believes that all she needs is a "chance to participate in community." The son's intellectuality and mother's sticky sentimentality cannot cope with Star's complete lack of civility. She causes a fight, and the son threatens to move to a hotel. In an effort to have the police take Star back into custody, Thomas plants a gun in her purse. This symbolic act fails, and he accidentally shoots his mother. Since this is the world of Flannery O'Connor, the story cannot be dismissed as a soap opera with a sad ending. In fact, some critics have suggested that the mistaken killing is Thomas's awakening and his mother's salvation.

Comforts of Home, like most O'Connor stories, is neither easy to take nor to understand. Although the plot sounds like a TV reject, the O'Connor touch transforms it into something almost cosmic. The film version is a thoroughly professional adaptation of the author's world of misfits, rejects, and imperfect communities.

40 minutes, color, directed by Jerome Shore. From Phoenix Films; rental also from Viewfinders.

The Concert

This short film, an Academy Award winner, is a "visual one-liner." Since London pedestrian crosswalks consist of wide white stripes painted on black roads, they resemble black-and-white piano keyboards. Comic Julian Chagrin uses this similarity to concoct a fantasy of a street musician (in the very literal sense) who works his musical magic on the pedestrian crosswalk behind London's Royal Albert Hall. As Chagrin jumps from white to black stripes, the soundtrack creates the illusion that the crosswalk has become the world's largest keyboard. A crowd gathers to marvel and enjoy, the local bobbies cooperate and conduct, a maintenance crew tunes up the pavement piano, and a good time is had by all, including the viewer.

The film, directed by Claude Chagrin, is a fine example of the simple idea well-executed. There are no wasted shots, no amateur cinematic ego trips.

12 minutes, color. From Pyramid Films; rental also from Viewfinders.

The Creditors

Before the days when feature films were made with one eye on the action and the other on potential television rights, the credits were shown before the film began. Often prosaic in manner, they nevertheless served the purpose of giving credit to the people who had made the film while allowing those at the end of the popcorn line to claim their seats before the action began. There was no need to involve an audience from the very first minute; the low admission fee of that era guaranteed an audience.

But once directors began to realize that their feature pictures would one day play on TV, they recognized that the credits would have to be presented in such a way that potential viewers would not switch channels. Today, you often find the setting of a film established and the plot already thicker than pea soup before the credits appear.

The Creditors is a spoof on this trend in feature films. It begins with a murder and then switches over to the credits. Viewers, who are not yet sure what they are watching, wait expectantly for the credits to end and the action to continue. It never does. Instead, there is an unending parade of the names of gaffers, assistant gaffers, and directors in charge of manicures.

In addition to credits, the film satirizes so many of the techniques of avant garde films that it would make an excellent programming choice for a film festival. The film was nominated for an Academy Award.

9 minutes, black and white, directed by Maxwell Myers. From Serious Business Co.

Dead Birds

"From 1496 B.C. to 1861 A.D., a period of 3,357 years, there were 227 years of peace and 3,130 years of war. This means that there were 13 years of war for every year of peace, and this is not a very heartening human record."

Donald Wells, The War Myth

Dead Birds is a reminder that man has perhaps always believed in war as a way to solve problems. The film is a documentary about the Dani tribes in Western New Guinea, a primitive people still living in the stone age. The Dani clans are in constant warfare, their territories divided by uncultivated strips of no-man's-land and their entire culture based on an elaborate system of intertribal killing and revenge.

When a warrior is killed in battle or when a raiding party fells a woman or child, the victors celebrate and the victims plan revenge. Each death must be avenged to satisfy the spirits and the ghosts of the slain tribal member. There is no conception of the possibility of war ever ending; it simply is a part of life, for without war how could the ghosts of the dead be satisfied? War also provides the Dani with a form of ritualistic excitement in what would otherwise be a tame, dull existence.

The film follows the Dani people in their daily lives, their constant patrols and watches, and into battle. It is 83 minutes long but comes on two reels for use in two group meetings if necessary.

Dead Birds raises the possibility that war is part of man's essential nature and will thus never be completely eradicated. The Dani culture can be compared to our own and found to have striking similarities in spite of the different levels of technological development. The film can also be used to illustrate how concepts of the spirit world and the afterlife tend to shape the actions of a culture. Many viewers will be amazed at how readily the Dani accept war as an inevitable, taken-for-granted part of life, yet their attitude seems little different from our own.

83 minutes, color, directed by Robert Gardner (1963). From McGraw-Hill Films and Phoenix Films; rental also from Viewfinders, University of California, and University of Michigan.

Dead Man Coming

Dead Man Coming is a documentary about San Quentin. Ken Ellis and Jeff Cohen were the first documentary filmmakers ever allowed inside this prison. They were promptly informed by the warden that if they were taken and held as hostages during the filming, the prison's policy would be to "declare their lives forfeit." The filmmakers not only survived their stay but managed to produce a documentary highly critical of the prison system yet avoiding many of the clichés of advocacy film journalism.

Prisoners, guards, wardens, and ex-prisoners bluntly express their opinions. The warden reminds viewers that "nobody ever got fired for failing to rehabilitate a man, but a hell of a lot of wardens have gotten fired for allowing people to escape." A guard sees clearly that "you don't start a revolution by killing a prison guard who makes $500 a month." After a lawyer doing time had organized inmates and informed them of their legal rights, he found himself classified as a psychotic and subjected to aversion therapy treatments. A prisoner ineptly interviewed ("How do you like it here?") answers the question, "How would you like to see things here changed?" with "Blow it up."

Prisoners talk articulately and persuasively of the dehumanizing effects of imprisonment. One reveals that parole comes only after the prisoner's buttocks have been stamped with a state of California stamp in black ink. They speak of living for years in an institution in which their every move is controlled and programmed. Freedom means being sent into the world without the ability to control one's own life.

Dead Man Coming is not a slick film, nor a typical liberal plea for prison reform. It is a film with rough edges that allows the prison to speak and forces the viewers to listen.

24 minutes, black and white (1973). From Pyramid Films; rental also from Viewfinders.

Death of a Peasant

This film is based on a true story of the last minutes in the life of a Yugoslav farmer in September of 1941. As the film opens, a group of peasants faces a German firing squad. One by one they are slaughtered in an open field probably once farmed by the victims.

But one man, not willing to die at the hands of the Germans, makes a running escape through a corn patch. The firing squad quickly finishes off the other victims and takes off after him on horseback. The chase sequence is very well constructed, using the cornfield as a dramatic setting much as Hitchcock did in *North by Northwest*. The horizon presents no refuge, only open fields where a man on foot can hardly hope to evade a squad of mounted soldiers. The peasant runs into a group of grazing cows, snatches a rope from one, and mysteriously nooses it around his own neck. Still running, with the Germans in close pursuit, he approaches a horse-drawn wagon, ties the free end of the rope to the wagon, and yells at the horses. When the soldiers close in, the horses leap forward, strangling the peasant as they drag him behind.

Viewers thinking in terms of a successful escape as they watch *Death of a Peasant* find the ending a shock. The peasant has escaped death at the hands of the enemy and died of his own free will— perhaps the ultimate freedom. He has defeated the enemy and affirmed human dignity in a hopeless situation. Some viewers will find his reasoning "dumb," whereas others will begin to see the self-inflicted death as a kind of final victory. An excellent film for discussion, as well as a finely made work for film study.

10 minutes, color, directed by Predrag Golubovic. From Mass Media Ministries; rental also from University of Michigan.

Directed by John Ford

When Orson Welles was asked which were his favorite American directors, he replied, "The old masters, by which I mean John Ford, John Ford, and John Ford." John Ford has directed nearly 140 films over the past 55 years, including American classics such as *The Grapes of Wrath, Stagecoach, The Informer, The Man Who Shot Liberty Valance*, and *The Last Hurrah*. So when the American Film Institute wished to produce a feature length film about a film director, Ford was the logical choice.

Directed by John Ford may be thought of as an anthology of film clips from the works of John Ford compiled by Peter Bogdanovich and structured around interviews with Henry Fonda, James Stewart, John Wayne, and Ford himself. Fifty-five excerpts from Ford films make up most of the film's 92-minute length. Although far from an in-depth study and perhaps a bit long, the film serves as a sort of cinematic museum exhibition devoted to a great director and his view of the West and American history.

The Fonda, Stewart, and Wayne interviews are scripted and staged to appear spontaneous, but they still work well. Bogdanovich deliberately staged them this way in order to invite comparison to the interviews by the reporter in *Citizen Kane* — for no apparent reason, but in keeping with the Bogdanovich style.

The film is best suited to groups seriously studying the American film or the works of John Ford. It is entertaining enough, however, to show to more general audiences.

92 minutes, color and black and white. From Films Inc.

Do No Harm

Since every eighth ad on TV is placed by a drug company, a documentary such as *Do No Harm* has little chance of gaining the wide televised exposure it deserves. The film takes a very critical look at the drug industry and reveals facts that a great many viewers will find shocking.

For example, doctors issue enough prescriptions to provide everyone in the U.S. with more than five drugs a year. Over two million people are hospitalized in one year from reactions to prescribed drugs. The drug industry spends an average of $4000 per physician in advertising and employs one "detail man" (salesman) for every ten prescribing physicians in the country.

The image of the doctor as an infallible worker of magic leads to patient expectations that are often unsatisfied *without* a prescription. The result is that 75 percent of all patients receive a prescription of some sort. Emotional problems are handled with pills to the extent that Valium is the number one prescribed drug. All this drugmania is encouraged by the multibillion dollar drug industry through advertising. Many doctors' knowledge of pharmacology from one or two courses in medical school is supplemented only by ads in the plethora of free medical magazines. Although the ads do spell out the effects of the drug in small print, their main effort is devoted to psycho-sell techniques similar to those used to sell beer and perfume.

Do No Harm suggests that patients should accept prescriptions only if they know what they are receiving. As one lady explains, "I will tell the doctor, 'I can't read your writing. What does this do, what is it for, and what are its effects?' " The film also points out that drugs prescribed generically often cost far less than brand-name prescriptions. The film suggests that the drug industry cannot be considered compatible with the profit motive if the nation is to be healthy instead of merely medicated.

Do No Harm ranges in technical quality from poor to average. Many of its interviews leave many questions unanswered. Although the film includes a spokesperson for the drug industry, it is very heavily biased. Nevertheless, its message desperately needs widespread preaching. Very useful for courses in health, consumer education, drug education, American problems, sociology, or advertising.

42 minutes, color (1975). From Serious Business Company; rental also from University of California.

Doubletalk

Doubletalk will prove an immensely successful education film because most viewers see a part of themselves in it; it makes them realize that their own problems with being honest and open with others are shared by nearly everyone.

The "plot" of the film is the mundane situation of a boy coming to pick up his date and getting stuck making small-talk with her parents while she dresses—hardly the stuff of high drama. But an overlapping soundtrack is used *sotto voce* to reveal the real thoughts of the characters. Their conversation is made up of the usual banalities while the thought-track reveals more profound, underlying tensions, disagreements, sarcasm, and distrust. The father offers the boy a drink in a simple verbal exchange. But the thoughts during those few seconds constitute a crash course in feeling out and checking the values of others.

The effect of the satire is funny, and audiences generally find the film a humorous entertainment. The overwhelming reaction to the film is, "That's the way it is—I've been there myself." Yet the lack of communication and underlying problems it exposes would be sufficient to keep any soap opera supplied with plot material for six months.

Only with a follow-up discussion of "why we laughed" will the film go beyond entertainment value. A viewing/discussion of *Doubletalk* can be useful for work in interpersonal communication or psychology. The film also lends itself well to workshop introduction and role-playing exercises.

9 minutes, color (1975). From LCA.

The Dove

The Dove has captured an Academy Award and numerous film festival prizes. I've seen it twice, both times in packed houses that reacted with a hilarity unlike that I've seen for any other short film.

The Dove opens with a serious tone and credits that indicate it is a Swedish Industries Production and has won the "Golden Escargot" of the Pan-European Film Festival. English subtitles are provided, and the plot at first seems similar to other Swedish feature films, especially those of Bergman. An aging professor is en route to receive a Nobel Prize and stops at his old house to relive memories.

After a few minutes, scattered snickers can be heard in the audience while more serious viewers quietly continue to puzzle out this exploration of existential anguish. But the laughter spreads as the audience gradually realizes that they have been taken. *The Dove* turns out to be a slapstick lampoon of Bergman.

The scenes and situations are all taken from various Bergman classics, the language spoken actually being a comical hybrid of English and Swedish-sounding suffixes. Viewers are so busy reading subtitles that they rarely notice the film is in English until it is halfway completed.

The fun of the film is in watching the truth slowly dawn on viewers. The more scholarly and accustomed to foreign films the audience, the better the reaction. Ideally, the audience should be wholly unsuspecting and perhaps even prepared for slaughter by a pompous introduction. A good audience laughs as much at its own gullibility as at the eventual slapstick humor of *The Dove*. A must for film societies, especially after a Bergman series.

15 minutes, black and white. From Pyramid Films; rental also from Viewfinders.

Eat, Drink and Be Wary

Eat, Drink and Be Wary is a hard-hitting, instructional film on our eating habits and the general degradation of food over the past twenty years. Cookbook author Anna Thomas emphasizes that convenience foods are tasteless compared to natural foods; nutritionist Dr. Jean Mayer points out that in our industrial society we have moved to a point where food is more "mined" than grown; and activist Michael Jacobson illustrates exactly how food processing destroys nutrition.

The film comes down hard on items like white flour, white and instant rice, sodium nitrate, an artificial food coloring known as "Red #2," and processed sugar. One of the most important points the film makes is that food advertising is largely responsible for the fact that one of the richest nations on earth is faced with a serious problem of malnutrition even among the affluent.

Eat, Drink and Be Wary is highly recommended for a study of nutrition, American problems, health, or the effects of advertising.

21 minutes, color. From Churchill Films; rental also from University of California.

Eggs

Eggs is a short animation film from the creative team of John and Faith Hubley. It opens with Fertility and Death riding together through the dawn in a speeding car. Fertility is happily and abundantly sowing the seeds of life while Death looks appropriately grim and skeletal. Death says to Fertility, "You're winning, but fifty or a hundred years from now you'll have to have a license to have a baby."

Cut to Martha and Harvey (a violinist by trade) as they apply for a license at the sperm bank. Martha pushes her shopping cart and makes selections to deposit in a huge machine. The machine rumbles away and out comes a baby—an expert violin player.

Meanwhile, back on the highway, Fertility threatens Death by saying, "They'll live forever."

Cut to a 200-year-old man reminiscing about his first heart transplant when he was a 52-year-old youngster. He drinks a toast to his original kidney and brings up the latest theory about having an identity crisis every hundred years or so, brought on by having so many parts of different people.

Back to the highway: Death threatens to push the button that would presumably end it all. Just before he does, "the chief" appears, a god-figure who sounds like a computer with emphysema. The "chief" inflates a "brand new planet" and gives Death and Fertility another chance and a few suggestions.

Eggs is entertaining, subtle, insightful, and an excellent discussion starter. It is suitable on some level with almost any audience.

10 minutes, color, animated. From Films Inc. and Film Images; rental also from Viewfinders.

Elegy

Elegy is a film parable about a prisoner who passes his time staring longingly at a red flower outside his cell window. He treasures and tries to protect it. The snow comes and covers the flower; the prisoner is angry but helpless. Finally, the flower comes back to life, and joy returns to the lonely captive.

As he enjoys the flower once again, a guard enters to release him, his sentence ended. On his way out he stands next to the flower, but now ignores it. He unfeelingly drops his suitcase on it, crushing the newly formed blossom, and walks away without a regret. The flower's value depended on its unavailability. Once within easy reach, its beauty was diminished.

Viewers will have varied interpretations of the film. Some will see the flower as representing freedom, valued only when lacking but taken for granted when possessed. Others will see the film in more general terms as a comment on how value is assigned to objects.

5 minutes, color, animation, directed by Nedeljko Dragic (1965). From International Film Bureau; rental also from University of Michigan.

The Emperor's New Armor

The Emperor's New Armor is a bit of witty and perceptive animation. The king in this parable is approached by Habadash Hardware, Ltd. and offered a new innovation in kingly dress: "soft armor." The three salesmen convince the king to buy the new outfit, but what they produce looks suspiciously like the old, traditional clanky armor. Nevertheless, the king accepts the armor and pays the bill for $113,000 (they tell him it's silver-plated). He clunks off in his new suit and sits down. He insists that he has soft armor, undaunted at having fallen through the chair, and torn dresses off the unprotected. Eventually, all his people are fitted with the new "soft armor" to protect themselves.

When the king's son arrives home from college, the father greets him with a hug. The son dies, with the father insisting that it's "just a little compound fracture." So ends the film. Moral? "In a world without armor, nobody is safe."

6 minutes, color, animation. From Pyramid Films; rental also from Viewfinders.

Empire of the Sun

Empire of the Sun is a student-made film that presents a California commune as a present-day Utopia. Sunburst Farm in the Santa Barbara mountains is the scene for this new-age commune whose members await the Second Coming. The film allows commune members to speak for themselves, but they all sound strangely as if they are either reading or reciting memorized lines. The commune farms for its livelihood and believes "with a little bit of compost and a lot of love we can grow anything." The film romanticizes communal life and is identical in style to thousands of films used to recruit boy scouts, marines, or nuns.

In spite of its naiveté *Empire of the Sun* is a very useful class film. It could be used as propaganda for the idea of communal living or to provoke pro and con discussion about the family. But because of its style the film serves best to illustrate the psychology of The True Believer. Birchites and communitarians, Jesus freaks and football fanatics all share certain traits that characterize the zealous believer in a cause or movement. Films made by True Believers, or films that allow only TBs to speak, share many of the same techniques. *More Than a School* is a True Believer film, as are most of the documentaries on Jesus People. According to Eric Hoffer, a student of The True Believer, "all mass movements generate in their adherents a readiness to die and a proclivity for united action; all of them . . . breed fanaticism, enthusiasm, fervent hope, hatred and intolerance; all of them are capable of releasing a powerful flow of activity in certain departments of life; all of them demand blind faith and single-hearted allegiance."

25 minutes, color (1974). From University of California.

The End of One

Paul Kocela spent a year observing the behavior of seagulls at New York beaches in order to obtain the right footage. His film shows a screeching mass of gulls fighting and feasting on a garbage dump while near the water's edge an older gull is left to die—alone and quietly. A loving attention permeates the film, making it a seven-minute masterpiece that has proved effective with both teen and adult audiences.

Besides being a work of art, the film is a cinematic Rorschach test, powerful in evoking feelings and many levels of interpretation. Some view the dying gull as abandoned by the other birds. Others say that the bird was poisoned by the garbage. Still others say that the film is a parable about life itself—civilization is a garbage heap that people fight over, unaware of the lonely ones who die away from the maddening crowd.

7 minutes, color. From LCA; rental also from University of California and University of Michigan.

Ersatz

Ersatz—adj. Substitute; artificial; especially an inferior imitation.

This Academy Award winning animation film from the Zagreb studios concerns the human tendency to substitute artificial substances for real ones, vicarious experience for the actual, and pseudo-character for virtue. The film's hero lives in a 100-percent inflatable world where the ideal woman can be made by blowing one up to just the right proportions, where a fish can be caught by blowing one up and throwing it into an equally inflatable instant lake. Even a shark can be inflated to "attack" the ideal woman so that rescue will help prove masculinity.

The hero's problem is that he is an ersatz person. He is in constant need of proving his real masculinity in spite of the readily available symbols of manhood. But in a world where all gratification is

E 49

instantaneous and a mere imitation, even a real man could not survive for long. Our hero finally meets with a stray tack and quietly hisses away into the fadeout.

The film is fine for a consideration of the "imitative," the "artificial," and the "vicarious" aspects of modern life—their dangers and values. A comparison between its inflatable world and our real one will turn up many similarities.

10 minutes, animation, color, directed by Dusan Vukotic (1961). From McGraw-Hill Films; rental also from University of Michigan and University of California.

Espolio

Buffy St. Marie and Joan Baez popularized in song the concept of the universal soldier. The NFBC short, *Espolio*, deals with the universal worker. The brilliantly drawn animation uses as script a poem by Earl Birney.

The speaker is the carpenter called upon to hammer onto the cross the criminal Jesus. He has a job to do: get the holes straight and deep enough to hold the spikes after they've penetrated the soft wrists. He has no time for the spoils or the soldier's dice games. Anyone can perform the indignities, but his skill is vital to the safety of the state.

As he works he muses that his sons will one day become carpenters "who'll build what's needed." Images flash by showing that what's needed ranges in time from cameras to guns, from pianos to guillotines, and from houses to bombs. A carpenter might one day be called to build a manger for a baby and later to nail that same baby to a cross. Anyone can kill and be killed, whether lynched by the Klan or slaughtered in an Asian hamlet, but only the skilled laborer can make the weapon.

The carpenter's words could give rise to guilt in workers who labor for firms who make missiles and tanks, or even those who pay the taxes to buy the bombs, crosses, or guillotines.

7 minutes, animation. From Films Inc.; rental also from Viewfinders.

An Essay on War

An Essay on War is a brilliant short essay by Emmy Award winner Andrew Rooney. The visuals are predominantly documentary footage with enough bombs, guns, killing, and explosions to please any audience with a normal degree of bloodthirst. The combination results in a highly watchable yet memorable exploration of man's attitude toward war.

Is war like an eclipse or flood, bound to recur periodically, or is it like some disease for which there might be a civilized cure? If we are really more civilized than those who have gone before, why then have we killed more than 70 million of our fellow human beings in this century? Perhaps it is because our killing is now done by remote control with the enemy only a statistic. The pictures of wife and children which soldiers carry in their breast pockets are destroyed along with them.

We no longer fight for mere land or plunder. We propagandize ourselves to believe that our war is for honorable and abstract reasons that even God Himself would surely bless.

We have become more proficient at killing. The scientists who invented the package of liquid fire and the engineers who designed a way to hurl it 50 miles probably love their wives and children and wouldn't hurt a butterfly. As quickly as we have learned to make something new, we have learned how to destroy it.

Rooney talks of the other reasons for our confusion and our passion for war and about the men who fight in the battles and frequently die. *An Essay on War* is one of the best written, most thought-provoking films on the subject.

23 minutes, color and black and white. From Encyclopedia Britannica Films; rental also from University of California and University of Michigan.

Eternally Yours

Swirling water, ominous music, and mysterious sounds pan in to a man's face that becomes a skull. A rescue squad leaves the fire station and arrives at the Pacific Ocean where it picks up the body and heads for a hospital. Medical equipment monitors the man's condition, a computer types out the state of his being—clinical, irreversible death. A sheet covers the body as it is taken down the elevator to the G level and the morgue. The body is cremated; ashes are swept into a box and taken to an airplane. The ashes are scattered over the ocean, and the film closes with a deus ex machina shot of a man rising from a golden sea.

Eternally Yours has the words "student film" written on every shot and splice, yet it manages to hold the viewer's attention through its details of the process of hospital death and despite its violation of dramatic expectations. There is no concern with who died, or how, or why, and no L.A. police homicide detectives arrive to shift attention from the corpse.

Eternally Yours could be used in death-education courses as an open-ended lead-in to the meaning of death, cremation versus burial, the symbolism of eternal life, the scientific determination of death, or even death as it normally appears in movies and on TV. The film is not of the best quality but serves as a refreshing change from the typical death-education film that focuses on the person about to die.

12 minutes, color, directed by Leopold Zahn. From Creative Film Society; rental also from Viewfinders.

Everybody Rides the Carousel

Everybody Rides the Carousel is a 72-minute animation created by John and Faith Hubley for prime-time telecast by CBS. The film takes viewers on the carousel of life through rides representing the eight stages of human growth proposed by psychologist Erik Erikson.

The film is a triumph of animation in the true sense of the word, it takes what could easily be a dull and uninspiring psychological exercise and brings it to life with believable characters and incidents that both entertain and instruct.

Fans of Hubley animations (*Windy Day, Eggs, The Hole*) will find much to enjoy in the style of drawing, the realness of the characters, and the universality of the situations. *Everybody Rides the Carousel* is the kind of film that any audience from ages 8 to 80 could enjoy. The eight stages of growth and the structure of the three-reel film are as follows:

PART I (24 min.)

Stage 1: The Newborn (trust and mistrust)
Stage 2: Toddlers (autonomy/shame and doubt)
Stage 3: Childhood (initiative and guilt)

PART II (24 min.)

Stage 4: School (competence and inferiority)
Stage 5: Adolescence (search for identity-leader/dreamer)
Stage 6: Young Adulthood (intimacy, love, friendship/loneliness, isolation)

PART III (24 min.)

Stage 7: Grown-ups (caring for the next generation/stagnation)
Stage 8: Old Age (integrity/despair; acceptance of death)

There is no voice-over narration in the film; each stage is illustrated by life situations. For example, a teenage girl argues with her parents about her plans to leave home, a couple struggles to express their intimate feelings openly about having a second child, an elderly couple faces death with dignity, a library security guard checks his tendency toward stagnation in order to help a young child, and a young couple discovers the meaning of love.

The film is quite useful to illustrate Erikson's theory and can generate considerable discussion if shown one part at a time. An audience that watches the entire film will very likely have seen so much as to be satiated rather than stimulated. The film is leisurely paced with the spots for commercial breaks all too evident. But this is a minor fault. *Everybody Rides the Carousel* is an excellent wedding of animation and life.

Each 24-minute part is available separately if desired.

From Pyramid Films; rental also from MMM, University of California, and Viewfinders.

Every Kid a Learner: An Alternative School That Works

The Independent Learning School in Corte Madera, California, is an alternative, but not a "free," school that is housed in two geodesic domes. *Every Kid a Learner* serves as an explanation of the philosophy of the school and shows the basics of its daily operation. The school takes students from ages 4 to 18, many of whom have had failing experiences in public schools, and teaches them responsibility toward themselves and others.

The school enjoys overwhelming success even as measured by traditional standardized tests. Yet there are no grades, no regular class periods, few class meetings, no classification of students as dyslexic, hyperactive, and the like. The ILS uses student teacher contracts, individualized learning, extrinsic rewards such as extra play time and field trips, frequent interaction among students, and a student-determined learning pace. The curriculum is fairly traditional and recognizes the need to prepare students for later life.

The operation of the school is based on the assumption that every kid is a learner if the learning environment is right for that kid. For example, a child who cannot sit still in a classroom might spend hours totally engrossed in some other activity. This is viewed as a case not of a short attention span, but of preference. The preference is used as a reinforcer to help the student learn.

Every Kid a Learner presents an attractive alternative to traditional schooling that is far removed from the "free school" movement. Many teachers and administrators will find ideas in the film that can be applied to traditional schools; others will be encouraged to know that such an alternative exists and works.

21 minutes, color, directed by Stephen Longstretch. A comprehensive printed guide accompanies the film. From Alternatives on Film.

The Eye Hears, the Ear Sees

This is a one-hour documentary on the work of Norman McLaren, excellent for film study, art classes, or any group familiar with McLaren's work. McLaren talks about his philosophy of art and how and why he makes films.

He explains that *Chairy Tale* expresses his own feeling that "I'm for the sat upon, the underdog, the exploited." He talks about the inspiration for several of his films, as well as the special techniques he has devised. The documentary contains numerous clips from McLaren films, including the uncut version of *Neighbors.* Almost all prints in circulation in the U.S. are "censored." In the original film one or both of the families of the two combatants are beaten. *The Eye Hears, the Ear Sees* shows this scene, although no mention is made of its widespread deletion.

McLaren demonstrates how his pixilation technique is accomplished in terms clear enough for anyone with a basic understanding of how film works to understand. Without some prior interest in McLaren and/or knowledge of film in general, the documentary is rather dull, but with this knowledge it makes for a fascinating hour.

59 minutes, color. From International Film Bureau and LCA; rental also from University of California and Viewfinders.

The Factory

Many short films document or sermonize about the dehumanizing conditions of factory work. *The Factory* takes viewers to a woodworking plant in northern California that uses "participatory management" to create an atmosphere in which workers can grow personally and management can show above-average profit and sales. Management treats all workers as honest and responsible unless proven otherwise and encourages their involvement in the decision-making process. Workers can call meetings to discuss factory problems; management offers workers flexible pay systems and asks advice on how to do certain jobs. When bidding on a project, management asks the workers what they are willing to accept as pay for this particular work. Individual initiative is encouraged, and a community spirit among the workers takes precedence over the need to keep a machine running at full capacity. Workers are allowed to be themselves; as one points out, "It's always exhausting to try to be what you aren't; and that energy isn't needed here."

The Factory is provocative in that it suggests simple, far from earth-shaking methods to humanize a work environment. Excellent for a study of institutions, work, or any situation in which there are bosses and subordinates. Visually, the film is far from exciting, and many of the workers' comments are of the cliché-generality variety. But The Factory does serve as a glance at an alternative that works. Related films include They Want to Make Work Human Again and Work.

26 minutes, color (1972). From Alternatives on Film; rental also from University of California.

The Family That Dwelt Apart

This film version of an E. B. White "Preposterous Parable," first written for the New Yorker in July of 1937, was nominated for an Academy Award as best animated short film. The dry, sardonic narration of White himself, the production of the National Film Board of Canada, and animation talent of director Yvon Mallette combined to make this gem deserving of both the nomination and the prize.

White's tale is of the Pruitt family living isolated from the rest of the world on their own island. The seven Pruitts are a nonconformist bunch not infected with the work ethic or the need for success. They sleep the winter away, celebrate the Fourth of July in their own private fashion, and are generally happy and utterly self-sufficient.

But one winter the bay freezes. The fact that they are "marooned" is quite all right with the Pruitts, the main drawback being that they can't go to shore to get the mail, "which was entirely second class" anyway. But the forces of civilization decide that the Pruitts need help. Help, to the Pruitts, is as welcome and beneficial as a pyromaniac would be to a fire department. The "rescuers" decide that one of the children needs an immediate appendectomy, and he is flown to the mainland. Another son is operated on at the island with details broadcast play-by-play over nationwide radio. The media attention brings more help, and with each addition the disaster quotient grows. Death by irony piles up. One Pruitt son expires from eating dried apricots that were airlifted to the island. The remaining Pruitts die from carbolic acid left by the surgeons. Only the Pruitt flown to the mainland survives the onslaught of do-gooders.

The film uses cartoon and kitsch elements of the late thirties from King Kong to Popeye to characterize each participant. E. B.

White narrates with a Death-Valley-dry tone perfectly matched to the black-humor irony of the "parable." The story is excellent for a discussion of do-gooding, intervention, self-reliance, media interference, irony, black humor, and matching of animation style to the story. Mallette's animation uses a wealth of ironic detail to further the mood of the film.

8 minutes, color, animated (1973). From LCA; rental also from University of California.

The Father

The Father is one of the best student films I've seen. The story is a twentieth-century update of Chekhov's *Grief*, a tale of an old man so alone he is unable to find anyone to share the grief of his son's death. Burgess Meredith turns in a superb performance as Captain Ned, who drives a horse and buggy around New York, hiring himself out for photographers and novelty rides through Central Park.

The film follows the old man around on New Year's Eve. At the beginning, he waits while an ad agency uses the horse and carriage as background for fashion photos. No one pays him. He attempts to tell someone about his son, Stephen Patrick, but no one wants to listen to an old man talk about family matters.

He picks up a fare at Lincoln Center and makes taxi driver chatter, always looking for an opportunity to tell of his grief. Near midnight a drunken party of four young people piles in his carriage and arrives at Times Square amid all its phony jubilance and ritualistic idiocy at the stroke of the new year. Back at the stable, a drunk offers no consolation. In the end, only his horse listens to his feelings.

Excellent cinematography and direction. A moving film touching the edges of the fear of death, aging, loneliness, and urban alienation in any audience. Also excellent as a study in translating literature to film.

28 minutes, black and white, directed by Mark Find. From New Line Cinema; rental also from University of California and University of Michigan.

Flatland

> "There is rarely a creative man who does not have to pay a
> high price for the divine spark of his great gifts."
>
> Carl Jung

The fate of visionaries, prophets, geniuses, or those who see through to the roots of problems is generally social rejection. A creature living in a two-dimensional world who suddenly discovers that there is a third dimension is subject to ridicule, charges of heresy, and, in Flatland, prison.

In *Flatland*, a world first envisioned by Edwin Abbot in the nineteenth century, there are only squares, triangles, and octagons. One little square receives a visit from a creature from another dimension—a sphere. Returning from his encounter with new concepts of depth, he finds himself unable to explain the added dimension in terms of Flatland vocabulary. Since there are no words to express the concept of 3-D, the frustrated square finds himself branded a radical nonconformist or a plain nut. From his two-dimensional jail cell, he continues to search for an explanation, convinced of his own experience, but unable to communicate his vision.

Flatland is fun to watch and can even be used in teaching math. An understanding of basic geometry is helpful in viewing the film but not essential. Its deepest meaning lies in its allegorical application to the Flatland of the mind.

12 minutes, color, animation. From McGraw-Hill Films; rental also from University of California and University of Michigan.

The Flight of Icarus

Gerald McDermott drew and animated this forthright telling of the myth of Daedalus and his son Icarus. The film simplifies the original myth somewhat but makes up in beauty of style what it lacks in plot detail.

The Flight of Icarus begins by telling of the great labyrinth Daedalus built for King Minos. When the work was completed, "the king was suspicious of the artist's knowledge" and cast him and his son into a prison of his own making. There they are threatened by mythic monsters and search for a way to escape. After Daedalus notices birds flying over the wall, he makes wings of feathers to fly away and over the sea. Icarus, against his father's warnings, soars up toward the sun and is destroyed. Unable to save him, Daedalus flies on to the shore and rests, grieving for his lost son.

The myth has discussion possibilities for topics such as the role of the artist, the daring of youth, or even the generation gap.

6 minutes, color, animated, directed by Gerald McDermott (1974). From Paramount Films.

The Fly

A real horror film stirs in its viewers a fear of something hidden in themselves. It enables them to see in themselves the Mr. Hyde of fiction, the oozing slimy things that crawl around the edges of feelings, the urges to kill or defile. Such inner visions are what chill the viewers. The only real monsters in movie houses are seated in the audience.

In the Zagreb animation, *The Fly*, viewers find themselves experiencing the irrational but common disgust with, and fear of, insects that verges on a national phobia. The fictional Dr. Hellstrom claims that insects are taking over the world, and those who see his filmed chronicle never put the word "only" before "bugs" again. Even if man isn't quite ready to abandon the planet to six-legged creatures, he certainly tries hard enough to keep his distance from the enemy. He tries so hard that his evasion can be explained only as a running from something within.

In the film, a rather immobile, ordinary man is pestered by a fly. Finally he gives in to his urge to kill and promptly steps on the pest. But the fly emerges from under his foot larger than ever. The fly grows and grows until it looms the equal in size of its would-be killer. The size perspective now reversed, the mammoth, despicable fly dive bombs its victim, coming closer with each pass. Its deep-throated buzz criss-crosses the screen, and finally the man is knocked into space. He floats to a gentle landing, unharmed and relieved to be rid of the menace. But here in this new world all the flies are his equal in size. One approaches and timorously places a hairy leg-arm around his shoulders. He responds with a similar friendly gesture, and the two learn to coexist in their mutual discomfort.

The Fly is not about insects. It is about fear, about being "bugged," about horror films, about ecology and man's relation to nature, about weakness, and even about death. It is a compelling and frightening film that is effective with audiences of any age.

9 minutes, color. From McGraw-Hill Films.

Frame-Up: The Imprisonment of Martin Sostre

In 1967 Martin Sostre operated three Afro-Asian bookstores in Buffalo, New York. This was a time of concern about "hot" summers in the nation's ghettos, and the police had Sostre tagged as one of the men responsible for much of Buffalo's trouble. Several days after a small riot, Sostre was arrested and charged with selling heroin. He was convicted and sentenced to 40 years in prison, where he remains today consistently claiming his innocence.

The prosecution witness who was involved with the drug transaction that convicted Sostre later changed his story and admitted that he took part in a set-up of the bookseller in order to lighten his own parole. But even this admission has failed to win Sostre a new trial. The film contends that Sostre was framed because of his political views and activity. Author Leslie Fiedler insists that the police used the cover of drugs to "maintain the political status quo." Tom Fleming of P.E.N. (the international authors' group) states that they are convinced that Sostre is a political prisoner.

In Sostre's appearance in the film, he tells of a visit to his bookstore by an agent of the FBI who told him, "You can get better stuff to sell than this 'Communist' stuff. If you're looking for trouble, that's all right with us." Sostre leaves viewers with the impression of a highly intelligent and articulate defender of his own Constitutional freedoms who has been victimized by those in authority. He tells of attempts to dehumanize him in prison through solitary confinement, frequent examinations, and arbitrary restrictions.

The truth behind the Sostre story is probably more complex than the film suggests. It is possible both that Sostre was set up and that he was a "substantial peddler" as the sheriff claimed. The value of *Frame-Up* is that it reveals exactly how easy it is for the "authorities" to use prisons as a form of political control to eliminate dissidents.

30 minutes, color, produced by Pacific Street Film Collective (1974). From Serious Business Company; rental also from University of California.

Frankenstein in a Fishbowl

This is Barry Pollack's absorbing, sad, and gruesome documentary about undergoing plastic surgery. The film follows two women through the preplanning conference with the doctor, the gory operation itself, and the recuperation and final evaluation of the job. At a recent showing to a class of high school girls, one became ill, one cried for 30 minutes, and all were 100 percent involved.

Millie is forty-four, fat, and wants a face lift. With a suave bedside manner, her surgeon explains the face lift process that will tighten up her face and leave only small scars around the ear. Hers is a sad situation because what she really needs is a decent diet and the will power to stick to it rather than a $2,000 face job that will enable her to continue to gorge candy. To improve her image, she unfortunately looks to doctors instead of to herself.

Pollack's *cinema verité* camera goes right into the operating room with Millie, and only those with a strong stomach will be able to watch the facial incisions and the lifting of the skin to stretch it taut. During the operation, the doctor calmly comments on what he is doing while most of the audience will shriek, groan, or simply look away from the bloody screen. Pollack doesn't seem to realize that a six-foot close up of a face being cut with scissors is more gruesome than the real thing.

Or perhaps he does realize, and this is just another of his cinematic weapons used to convince viewers that plastic surgery is sad, cruel, and definitely not for the sane. His use of extreme close-ups and glaring lighting as well as his general selection of shots and editing definitely convey his disdain for the whole subject. The film, as the title hints, is both a behind-the-scenes look at a fascinating and rarely publicized subject and a polemic against its absurdity.

The second lady in the film receives a nose job to smooth down the hump in her nose. The scenes of the operation are even gorier than those of Millie's.

Frankenstein in a Fishbowl is a bit too long, and much of the conversation between the two women in the hospital during their recovery is hindered by all the bandages. When the bandages finally come off, both women look as if they had been on the losing side of a roller derby riot, but eventually the swelling and bruises heal. Millie looks duly plastic, whereas the other has indeed a straight nose. Millie comments that she probably wouldn't do it again—"It's not that rewarding"—but the other already is considering smoothing off some of the point from her chin.

Frankenstein in a Fishbowl is an engrossing film for almost any audience, excellent for values confrontation and discussion as well as for illustrating cinematic techniques aimed at visual persuasion.

43 minutes, color. From Time-Life Films; rental also from University of Michigan.

Frank Film

Frank Film, though brilliant in technique, has few of what might be called "socially redeeming qualities." It has garnered more prizes on the film festival competition circuit than any other short film in memory. At latest count, it had won twelve first place awards alone, consistently standing far above the competition. This is partly because of the lack of competition, but also because of filmmaker Frank Mouris's virtuoso performance. You see, *Frank Film* isn't about frankness; it's about its creator.

Frank Mouris had been saving images, mainly from magazines, for five years, "just because I like them." He has taken these thousands of images to flash across the screen while he narrates his singularly unexciting autobiography. Such is the stuff of terrible amateur films, but this time it becomes a cinemagraphic calling card, a "look ma, no hands" boast by a fellow with a superb sense of graphic design.

The film is fresh, totally engrossing, a marvel of technique. Anyone who has experimented with making films from stills and cutouts will be convinced that Mouris is part filmmaker and part magician.

Frank Film is a portent of the animation of the future. Don McLaughlin started it all with his kinestatic *God Is Dog Spelled Backwards*, Charles Braverman cashed in on it with *American Time Capsule* and other films, but Frank Mouris makes these efforts look amateurish by comparison. His soundtrack is an equally creative blend of straight narrative and stream of consciousness.

9 minutes, color. From Pyramid Films; rental also from University of California, University of Michigan, and Viewfinders.

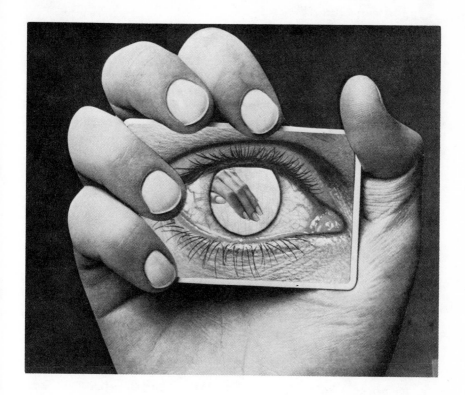

The Further Adventures of Uncle Sam

Take Uncle Sam, a bald eagle, and the Statue of Liberty, put them in Cartoonland, give them the archetypal American plot of villain-hero-maiden-in-distress, and you have *The Further Adventures of Uncle Sam*.

This nostalgia-camp-satire-adventure cartoon is a pastiche from Disney, Lance, Terry, *Yellow Submarine*, and comic book art. Uncle Sam, who runs a gas station, is abducted by a group of Blue Meanie types who think in $$$ and threaten to blow him up. But his faithful

sidekick, the bald eagle in tennis shoes, rescues him. While Sam and the eagle are occupied elsewhere, the Meanies kidnap the Statue of Liberty, which desperately clings to Yellow Pages. Sam and the eagle speed to her rescue in a blimp, passing over a gory tableau of the American dreamscape. Such realities, however, are not the concern of our mythical heroes.

Meanwhile, back at the ball park, Liberty is tied to a red, white, and blue barber pole while a detestable villain prepares to blow her up to entertain the cheering crowds. But the eagle carries off the bomb in the nick of time, and all three go off into the sunset, presumably to live capitalistically ever after.

15 minutes, color. From Pyramid Films and Creative Film Society; rental also from Viewfinders.

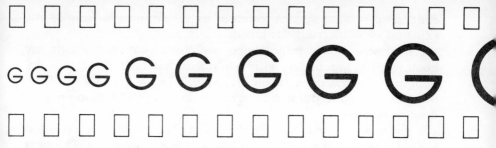

Garden Party

Garden Party is an impeccable cinematic adaptation of the much-studied Katherine Mansfield short story of the same name. It is the story of Laura, a southern teenager from the upper crust of plantation society who is initiated into the mysteries of poverty and death. Laura is a big, gay, naive, over-protected but sensitive girl who is quite upset when she hears of a fatal auto accident involving a neighbor. She believes that the closeness of the death is cause enough to cancel that afternoon's scheduled garden party. But her mother and sister brush her views aside and explain that the world can't stop every time someone dies.

After the party Laura is asked to carry the leftovers next door to the grieving family. There, in harsh contrast to the luxury and party atmosphere, is the sorrowful widow, the fatherless family, and the earmarks of poverty. Laura is shown the corpse, neatly laid out on an upstairs bed.

The realization that a party can take place at the same time that a dead person is mourned nearby is a profound and mysterious discovery for Laura. She cries yet declares to her older brother, who assumes that the experience must have been "awful," that the dead man looked so peaceful, almost beautiful." As in Katherine Mansfield's story, the film ends with its most important themes still simmering below the surface, inviting meditation and discussion.

The Garden Party was changed slightly from the original to improve its visual impact. The screen adaptation ranks as one of the best I've ever seen in short films. The film reveals high technical and artistic standards, even down to detailed period costumes and props. The acting is excellent; the cinematography, simple and fitting.

24 minutes, color, directed by Jack Sholder (1973). Rental also from University of California and University of Michigan.

Getting Married

Charles Braverman contracted with ABC-TV to produce a 90-minute documentary on marriage in America. The film was aired as a late night special; now a shortened version is available from Pyramid. The condensed version spends much of its 29 minutes looking at the exploitation of marriage for profit.

In case a viewer might have any doubt that marriage is big business, the film begins with reminders that 1,800,000 autos are bought by newlyweds each year, $125 million is spent on formal wear, $358 million on wedding photography, and over $2 billion on wedding receptions.

Viewers are given a quick tour of marriage kitsch at a fashion show for prospective brides run like a Tupperware party. The next stop is the wedding center of the U.S.A.—Las Vegas. There, in Nevada's neon oasis, 50,000 couples a year are married, giving the grateful city $60 million in revenue.

A ten-minute wedding in a Las Vegas "chapel" is shown while the operators assure the viewers that they are interested primarily in preserving the sacredness of marriage. A brief interview with the newly married couple devastatingly reveals that this particular marriage is unlikely to last the trip back home to parents in California. To lure prospects, a "quick serve wedding joint" offers free pizza, beer, and a roll of slot machine nickels with every marriage.

Those lucky enough to survive Las Vegas with cash intact can then fly straight to the Pocono Mountains where numerous resorts await to serve them. The film gives a glimpse of Cove Haven, a honeymoon resort famed for its 150 heart-shaped bathtubs.

The film concludes positively with a look at marriage as an age-old ceremony filled with meaning, joy, and love. A Jewish wedding is briefly shown, emphasizing its mixture of tradition and modernity.

As a film, *Getting Married* is obviously a "condensed version." It suffers from a lack of consistent viewpoint. There is no doubt, however, that it is thoroughly entertaining and could be used to discuss what marriage means and how it is best celebrated.

29 minutes, color, directed by Charles Braverman (1976). From Pyramid Films; rental also from University of California.

Good Country People

Only a reader familiar with the world of Flannery O'Connor could read a plot summary of *Good Country People* and understand that it is not a story from *Modern Romances*. Hulga is a sullen, 36-year-old woman with a Ph.D. in philosophy, a bad heart from a childhood hunting accident, a wooden leg, and a view of life gained entirely from books. She lives on a farm with her mother and seems to have no interest in life.

But along comes a bumbling Bible salesman who endears himself to Hulga's mother by explaining that he's "just a country boy" and reassuring her that "good country people are the salt of the earth."

Hulga and the salesman hate each other right off but are able to form a strange bond (in the world of O'Connor, all personal relationships are "strange") based on the shared belief that they both might die.

He invites her on a "picnic walk in the woods," and Hulga accepts, being too naive to realize that the Bible salesman is a con man out to take advantage of her by rules other than those in the Bible. They climb into a hayloft, where he slobbers her with kisses and insists that she admit she loves him. About love Hulga explains, "It's not a word I use, I don't have illusions. I'm one of those persons who sees through to nothing. We are all damned. Some of us have taken off our blindfolds and see there is nothing to see — it's a kind of salvation." In Hulga's economy, it is the Bible salesman who is damned and she who is saved. Perhaps it is out of pity that she allows him to kiss her and admits finally that she loves him "in a sense." He asks her to "prove it" by showing him her artificial leg because "it's what makes you different."

She shows him. He takes the leg off, hugs it, and hides it in his suitcase along with his pornographic playing cards, whiskey, and parts of other people. As he explains, "I one time got a woman's glass eye this way." He abandons Hulga in the hayloft, legless, and emptied even of her emptiness. His parting line after the ultimate con is "Hulga, you ain't so smart. I've been believing in nothing ever since I was born."

32 minutes, color, directed by Jeffrey F. Jackson (1975). From the filmmaker, 29023 View Drive, Agoura, Calif. 91301.

The Good, Good, Good, Good Life

This film is a general critique of what is often called the "life-style of conspicuous consumption."

A retired older man works quietly and contentedly at a potter's wheel. But the peace of creation is broken by his daughter and son-in-law, who arrive in a Winnebago and explain that they've heard he is going to marry a nearby widow. The daughter, who seems to enjoy stroking a coffee pot inordinately, tells her dad of all the wonders of modern life that he could have. With their smiles exceeded in plasticity only by their credit cards, the two deluge the old man with appliances and completely redo his old-fashioned but homey living room. His son-in-law even makes a pitch for "Indian Village," a housing development for couples in their "golden years." But father knows what is best and kindly but firmly rejects their intrusion.

The film is made in the style of a TV commercial with all the usual insanity—singing and dancing about coffee pots and vacuum cleaners. It is oversimplified in its presentation of values but even so allows those in the audience who prize above all their electric garage door openers to both laugh and ponder. *The Good, etc., Life* is fun to watch, yet might make viewers a bit more aware of how much our consumer life-style costs in terms of human lives, pollution, waste, and debilitation of spirit and ingenuity.

11 minutes, color, directed by Rolf Forsberg (1974). From Tele-Ketics.

Good Night Socrates

On the surface this fine student-made film by Maria Moraites and Stuart Hagman (who later made the feature film *The Strawberry Statement*) is about the destruction of an old Greek ghetto in Chicago. On a deeper level it is about culture shock, the survival of tradition, and Christian symbolism in modern life.

A boy is present when his aunt and grandfather receive a forty-day eviction notice that signals the beginning of the end of "Greek town." The film ends on Easter Saturday, when the boy and his family must leave their home on Socrates Street. At Greek services that day, the boy comes to understand what death and resurrection mean and what Easter is all about.

Every shot in the film is carefully composed and reverberates with symbolic meaning. The "Funeral—No Parking" sign on the sidewalk refers to the demise of the neighborhood and the only way of life as well as the absence of a place to park. The forty-day eviction notice and the forty days of Lent have symbolic meaning, as do the meeting with the American boy on the merry-go-round, the old man who sits by the olive tree, the seemingly free pigeons, and the many gates observed throughout the course of the film.

The film's overall theme is that progress is painful but that the young can find resurrection in what the oldsters see only as death. The film has little narration, relying mainly on the poetry of its camerawork.

Good Night Socrates can be used in a study of the value of tradition, the idea of cultural death and resurrection, Christian symbols, the Greek Orthodox religion, and the attitude of different generations toward change. It also illustrates the idea of "future shock."

34 minutes, black and white, directed by Maria Moraites and Stuart Hagman (1962). From Northwestern University Film Library.

The Guns of Autumn

This 77-minute news documentary is one of the best films to come along in years for the study of bias, point of view, and emotional persuasion. It is also one of the best documentaries on hunting as a sport.

The Guns of Autumn takes viewers to five hunts around America. Nearly tame black bears are shot in a garbage dump near a small Michigan town on the opening day of the season; elsewhere a bear is treed with the help of cars, walkie-talkies, dogs, and at least a dozen hunters; thousands of water-fowl are shot in a game management area set up to control the size of the flock; buffalo are shot by Arizonans who pay $160 to $500 for a permit that guarantees them a kill; and exotic animals for trophy rooms are hunted in a private fenced preserve where the hunter always gets what he wants.

The documentary shows "sport" hunting as an activity that is often devoid of any resemblance to the traditions of sport or hunting. Instead, it has become a two-billion-dollar-a-year industry that requires of its participants all the skill and sporting ability of a carnival rube trying to win a stuffed animal at a shooting gallery. The film pays lip service to true sportsmanship by at least interviewing a woman who hunts with bow and arrow and who admits that she has yet to bag her first prey.

But *The Guns of Autumn* devotes the bulk of its time to the hunter armed with technology and the help of game wardens or businessmen who control hunts so that the odds are entirely on the side of the hunter. The buffalo hunt in Arizona has all the excitement of picking out a frozen steak in the supermarket, yet the "hunters" are thrilled with their trophies. The "hunt" on the private game ranch takes place in one square mile of fenced land crowded with more animals than the Chicago zoo. Even in such an environment, a hunter needed five shots to kill his deer and was left huffing and puffing by his 13-minute ordeal.

The film shows animals being shot and dying; there are no fade outs on the kill as in programs such as "The American Sportsman." Some critics contend that showing the blood and guts and concentrating only on the aberrations of hunting make this a highly biased documentary. But producer-director Irv Drasnin defends his film as one that "did not say anything good or bad about hunting, but let the hunter speak for himself." He asks rhetorically, "Would we have been better reporters if . . . we had faded out on the gunshot when in fact the story does not end there? Wildlife bleeds and dies, animals are gutted, carcasses are carried off, hung to cool, and displayed with pride in the field and in the home."

The Guns of Autumn does show the social life of the hunter and does allow hunters to explain why they hunt. Ironically, those who respond evade the question and talk about being a part of nature and enjoying the outdoors. These answers, of course, could apply to birdwatching, golfing, or hiking; the hunters fail to deal with the idea of death and guns. None admit that they hunt because they enjoy killing. In fact, the hunters use euphemisms such as "bagging" or "harvesting" animals and less often speak simply of "killing" them. There are traces of self-deception evident in these interviews, and very likely they were selected with this in mind.

The Guns of Autumn is biased in a subtle way, a way that makes the film true yet provocative. An excellent review of it can be found in the Nov./Dec. 1975 issue of *Columbia Journalism Review*. The Jan./Feb. 1976 issue carries a reply by the director of the film. Highly recommended.

77 minutes, color (1975). From Carousel Films; rental also from University of California.

Gym Period

"After three years some of you haven't made it to the top yet," the crew-cut gym teacher tells his class of high school boys. The ropes swing silently in the small, sunlit gym as the boys scramble once again to prove their ability and, one suspects, their fragile masculinity. The kids average seven to nine seconds to reach the top, while the others cheer and generally act like high school kids in a gym class. But to Jerome the rope climb has been a source of failure for three years; again he struggles to reach the top but stops short and descends humiliated. The class groans and quickly forgets about him in a game of throwing rubber balls at each other.

While the class plays its own version of survival of the fastest, another student enters the gym to practice on the parallel bars. Dressed in white and looking older and more suave than the others, he is no doubt the school gymnastics hero. Jerome watches him practice and waits until class is over. Then, in the gym empty except for the figure on the parallel bars, Jerome tries again to climb the rope. Only a few feet away from the top, he grunts, groans, and falls as the bell rings, signaling the next period.

Gym Period is a good film about striving for a goal, about realizing limitations, and about living with failure in the face of a group. But filmmaker Nicholas Frangakis struggles to give the event cosmic meaning, like Phineas's fall from the tree in *A Separate Peace*. The more the film is stretched for theological meanings (the boy in white on the parallel bars makes an embarrassing Christ), the less interesting the film becomes, and the more its weaknesses show. But as a film with psychological meaning, *Gym Period* is definitely worth a careful viewing and discussion.

10 minutes, color (1975). From TeleKetics.

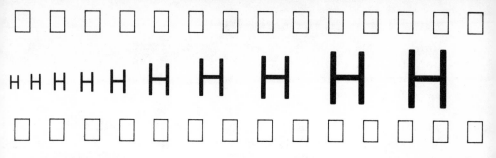

The Hand

> "The hand is a force which compels each individual to do what he does not wish to do. Like a thread there runs through history something one might define as an institution, convinced that its truth is universal truth, clamoring for attention and insistent on being considered right by everyone. The man is a mask which may conceal any human face, a person of indeterminate occupation and age. It never changes. Only his expression is dictated by given situations."
>
> *Jiri Trnka, maker of* The Hand

The Hand is a powerful animated allegory that has become one of the most popular classroom films of the past five years. A puppet man is the film's central character, his antagonist a huge powerful hand that tries to threaten him into sculpting hands instead of flower pots. The potter refuses, but the hand persists in its threats until the man has been roped, caged, and forced to chisel out of stone a huge image of the enemy hand.

Although the man escapes, he eventually meets with a tragic, ironic, and absurd end in his futile efforts to elude the hand. The hand discovers the potter's corpse, carefully places it in a coffin, arranges for a funeral, and concludes the film with a chilling black glove salute.

Every viewer has a "hand" in his or her own life; many viewers are "hands" in the lives of others. The film is most effective when its meaning is interpreted on a personal level, which can be in many ways, including explanations dealing with art, totalitarianism, religion, and society.

19 minutes, color, animation, directed by Jiri Trnka (1965). From McGraw-Hill; rental also from Viewfinders.

Hard Times in the Country

Hard Times is a solid NET investigative report on the American food industry. Commentary and interviews with farmers quickly show that rising food prices are not caused by greedy farmers. In fact, the small farmer is being driven into the city.

As is often the case, federal legislation disguised as a means of "helping" a nearly powerless segment of society is in reality a means of suppression. Farm subsidies have a regressive effect, with the 20 largest farmers receiving more money than the smallest 300,000. The top men have Congressional representation; in fact, in 1969, Senator Eastland of Mississippi received a $117,000 farm subsidy. Since subsidies began, over 50 percent of small and medium sized farmers have been forced off their land. The U.S. is losing an average of 100,000 farmers per year.

Farming has given way to the 100-billion-dollar-a-year food industry. A few corporations control it; the top 50 food manufacturers make more profit than the next 30,000. A&P, Kroger, Safeway, and Acme account for 50 percent of urban food sales. Kellogg makes double the national average return on its investment. Campbell sells 85 percent of all soup in the country.

The food processors pay low prices for natural farm food and turn it into high-priced pseudo-food. A consumer group is shown squeezing a loaf of Wonder Bread that truly deserves the adjective "wonder," since without air it almost magically disappears into a lump of goo.

The film goes behind the story of rising food prices that is superficially reported in the newspapers since newspapers are dependent on the food industry for advertising income. *Hard Times in the Country* is a solid documentary with a point of view not often seen in the media.

58 minutes, color. From Indiana University; rental also from University of California and University of Michigan.

Harmony

Harmony is a comic animated film from Romania that questions traditional male and female roles and the integrity of the individual who plays these roles.

As the film opens, a man and wife emerge from an apartment. Each assumes the conventional role that society expects—the man strong and aggressive and the woman weak and passive. The two arrive at their office. He is the high-powered executive who demands complete obedience from his subordinates. His wife is a timid, terrified clerk-typist who does only menial work and quivers when she is called on the carpet by her boss-husband.

But when the two return home, their roles reverse completely. She domineers now, and he meekly dons an apron to sweep, clean, and cook. What the title ironically calls "harmony" is in reality a dehumanizing puppet-like existence in which both act out parts having little to do with wholly realized human lives. Their apartment door represents the boundary line between one's public and private face. *Harmony* claims that the more exaggerated and unnatural the individual's life must be outside the door, the more he or she must compensate by contrary behavior behind the door.

8 minutes, color, animated by Horia Stefanescu. From Wombat Films.

Harold and Cynthia

Harold and Cynthia explores the impact of advertising on people. Harold and Cynthia are two ordinary people who meet at a bus stop and are attracted to each other. But their attempts to establish a relationship are distorted by Madison Avenue messages that tell them that importance and value are to be measured by the corporate products they use and the media ideals they conform to.

The simple animation changes to live action to present the actual commercials that Harold and Cynthia see: "Smoke this and win the girl of your dreams"; "Spray on a little of this and he'll follow you anywhere."

Harold and Cynthia have difficulty getting in touch with themselves or each other. The simple animation style conveys perfectly the emptiness of their world. Only when they go to a place where there is no advertising does the animation style become fuller, and they are able to dance and to express joy and tenderness. Many viewers will consider the ending a bit overdone, since advertising, although a factor contributing to alienation, is hardly the sole cause.

The sound track uses "appropriate" pop tunes unobtrusively— "Sounds of Silence" is done with a solo flute. The film is bound to have some appeal to almost any audience and makes its point clearly and with visual interest.

10 minutes, color, animation. Rental from Viewfinders.

The Hole

There currently exist 28,000 pounds of explosives for every man, woman, and child on the face of the planet. All this power acts as a force to keep the peace—such is the current state of international affairs. In fact, bombs tend to explode sooner or later, on purpose or by accident.

In *The Hole*, the talented animation team of John and Faith Hubley explore the possibilities of accidental nuclear war. Two workers in an excavation begin to argue about the cause of accidents on the job. One believes that carelessness is the villain, while the more suspicious argues that accidents are subconscious expressions of the will to self-destruction. The highly intellectual but fascinating debate turns from job injuries to nuclear war, only to be interrupted by the crash of a piece of falling machinery. The two workers climb out of the hole, expecting to be the sole survivors of an atomic blast. They are relieved, but for how long?

Winner of an Academy Award for best cartoon short, *The Hole*, is useful for a discussion about the arms race and the use of force to keep the peace. The film suggests that it doesn't really matter if an atomic explosion is an intentional act, a careless accident, or a hidden expression of the death wish.

It should be noted that poor acoustics in a viewing room will render parts of the dialogue difficult to understand.

10 minutes, color, animation, directed by John and Faith Hubley (1962). From Films Inc.; rental also from University of California, University of Michigan, and Viewfinders.

Homo Augens

"Homo augens" translates as "man growing" and serves as an ironic title for this nightmarish Zagreb animation. The protagonist awakens and looks out his apartment window to see people stream into the city streets like blood in human veins. He finds a female and devours her. Her bones clutter the room. He grows in size and looks more like King Kong than a man as he slams through a wall to stalk the city. He eats more and more people, grows with each feast, and eventually towers above buildings. But his rampage proves to be his own destruction; he leaves the city holding his head in pain and falls dead in its outskirts.

Morning dawns and all seems normal; again people swarm into the city. Soon crowds gather around the fallen monster and form lines to pass along great chunks of his body, loading them onto meat trucks, until only his massive skeleton remains. The camera pulls back to reveal other skeletons littering the outskirts of the city.

Homo Augens may be viewed as a *Soylent Green* nightmare, a surreal dreamscape, a story about city life and progress, or a metaphor of society or life in general.

Superb Zagreb animation, a clear story line, and the fascination that attracts viewers to horror shows should make this a popular film for the strong of stomach.

9 minutes, color, animation (1972). From BFA.

Horse Latitudes

In 1957, nine men set out individually to become the first to sail around the world alone, nonstop. One of the boats, the trimaran *TIA*, was found by a passing freighter months later, adrift and deserted in mid-Atlantic. Aboard the boat was a log that told a story that would rival Conrad's *Heart of Darkness*, with the one exception that the story of the log really happened. *Horse Latitudes* is a dramatic recreation of the fate of Philip Stockton, a middle-aged braggart yearning for fame and adulation, when he attempted to sail around the world aboard the *TIA*.

Stockton sets out late in the race, hoping to catch the eight others with the superior speed of his trimaran. Instead, he finds that his boat "leaks" from above and requires frequent bailing, and that the calm of the "horse latitudes" makes even a fleet sailboat helpless. He decides to keep a duplicate log, a "Devil's log," that will fake his progress. This would enable him to drift for a while in the south Atlantic and then head home without sailing around the dangerous waters of the Cape. But his conscience is troubled, and he worries about accepting a cash prize for a faked victory, thus opening himself to the crime of fraud. He finally decides to come in second and accept only the praise and publicity rather than the money. After drifting calmly and making up exciting adventures that never happened, he learns by radio that all the other contestants have dropped out; he now cannot come in second. Thus, the conflict of man versus the sea changes to that of man against himself. Stockton is faced with living with the whole world knowing of his fraud or with the whole world, except one, believing him a hero.

His mind begins to weaken in its isolation and the quiet of the horse latitudes. In a half-sane mood, he decides that his boat is loaded with too much baggage for one man to carry around the world. He starts throwing things overboard and finally decides that he is not willing to push himself any further. He jumps overboard knowing that he himself is the source of the evil he faces.

Horse Latitudes is well-produced and acted. Its pacing is a leisurely 43 minutes that could have been better used to develop Stockton's character more fully and reveal more of the nature of his torment. Although imperfect, the film is still superior to most short films and should serve well for discussions of values, conflict, honesty, and suicide. The film could also be compared to works of literature, by Conrad and Ionesco, for example, that treat similar themes.

43 minutes, color, directed by Peter Rowe (1976). From Wombat Films; rental also from Viewfinders.

How Could I Not Be Among You

This is a film portrait of Ted Rosenthal, a poet who has been told he has leukemia and will live for only six months. The mixture of stills and cinematography blends nicely with the narration, which consists mainly of Rosenthal's own poetic thoughts on the approach of death. First shown two years ago on *Great American Dream Machine*, the film has a grace and power rarely found in short films.

Some of Rosenthal's comments: "I was dying according to a pattern—the pattern of terminal cancer patients; they predicted how I would feel and they were right. I didn't have a self-image to worry about, nothing I had to be, and I felt free; I could leap out the window for the fun of it. At first I called people and told them, 'Guess what, I'm dying'; this felt good, immediate and complete sympathy. Once you have nothing, you can be anything. I think dying is not different than being born. I don't think people are afraid of death; they're afraid of the incompleteness of their life. I'm sick of dying, it's a drag, makes me depressed. I was a happier person when I became sick. Life is grim, but not necessarily serious. Never yearn for your past, your childhood is worthless, there is no escape in Christmas, no fantasy will soothe you, you must open your heart and expect nothing in return, return to your simple self."

The 30-year-old Rosenthal's poetry is both tough and tender and often reminiscent of Ferlinghetti. As the film ends, he is still living as a man who knows death, perhaps to be cured, perhaps soon doomed.

28 minutes, color, directed by Thomas Reichman. From Benchmark Films; rental also from University of California, University of Michigan, and Viewfinders.

Hunger

A Peter Foldes film is always an event for the student of animation; Foldes was one of the most creative animators in the 1970s. In *Hunger*, Foldes shows that computer animation can offer more than dazzling progressions of geometrical shapes. In fact, his use of the computer is so subtle that many (perhaps most) viewers will be unaware that a machine contributed to the animation process.

In *Hunger*, Foldes further develops his favorite image of man the devourer. The protagonist of this film is a businessman shown eating at restaurants, buying food in a deli and a supermarket, entertaining a female pick-up with a meal at home, and finally retiring for the night, a bloated but supposedly satisfied creature. When this man eats, he turns into a mouth and gathers into himself whole pigs and other single-swallow dinners. He does not eat to live; he lives to eat—a voracious consumer of all that is placed before him. Underlying his appetite is his view of women as creatures also made for man to devour. But in *Hunger*, Foldes allows this theme to remain secondary.

After the gorbellied creature dozes off to a stuffed sleep, he has a nightmare in which he falls through darkness before landing among

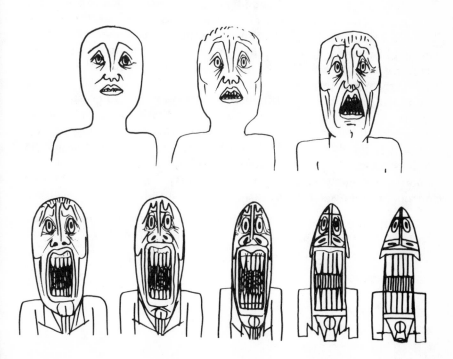

the starving people of the world. Their rib cages show their bones, and their eyes are widened by hunger. Our bloated hero lies in their midst, and they fall upon him to survive. A crude but fitting justice is served.

Ultimately, *Hunger* is a film about a world in which 2 percent of the population consumes 40 percent of the resources.

11 minutes, color, directed by Peter Foldes (1974). From LCA; rental also from Viewfinders.

The Hunt

The Hunt is an eerie, frightening, and ambiguous film—part allegory and part horror story. It begins in the middle of some conflict, perhaps a civil war, that is never explained to the viewer. A long-haired young man, tattered and wounded, is running through a wooded area. He is chased by four or five men on horseback. Finally exhausted, he drops within sight of an old white-bearded frontiersman chopping wood, who takes him into his cabin and cares for him with almost motherly tenderness.

Not a single word is spoken throughout the entire film, an occasional solo flute providing the only musical backdrop. An element of suspense keeps the audience glued to every movement the man and boy make—yet nothing to speak of happens. The nothingness, however, is laden with some kind of foreboding significance.

The man goes out to shoot a bird and brings it back to prepare it for eating. The boy watches, cries, and walks away into the woods. The man watches him through the window, and soon the black-clothed horsemen appear on the horizon. They ride up to the house, bringing back the boy. The old man sticks a knife in his belt and steps forward. End of film.

Is the film about cannibalism? About some strange society in which there are the hunters and the hunted? About a psychological process? Is it based on some well-known short story? I'm not sure, yet I found it totally involving and visually rich. It is valuable for its understatement, its purely visual approach to storytelling, and its sense of strangeness. Its ultimate ambiguity might be a bit too much for most audiences, but as a literary adventure it is worth a grapple.

25 minutes, black and white, directed by University of Texas student, Thomas Roberdeau. From Pyramid Films.

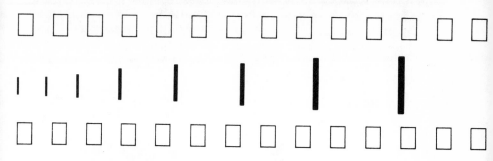

I. F. Stone's Weekly

I. F. Stone's Weekly should be shown to all students of mass media in the hope that it might inspire the reporters of tomorrow to emulate the clarity, toughness, official skepticism, and humility of Isadore Feinstein Stone.

I.F. Stone is an investigative newman who started his own newsletter in response to a McCarthy era blacklisting. *I.F. Stone's Weekly* grew to a 1969 circulation of 70,000 when Stone finally retired at the age of 64. Today, he writes occasional pieces for the *New York Review of Books.*

Stone's first assumption is that "every government is run by liars"; his second is that "a government always reveals a great deal if you really take the trouble to study what it says." Newspapers that print largely what is given out by official sources "act as the unwitting propaganda arm of the government." While Stone talks about the establishment reporters and the purpose of the media as "merchandising," the film shows a few seconds of tennis between then press secretary Ron Ziegler and an ABC reporter. The private White House courts appear inviting, and even Tricia Nixon looks on smilingly. With this transposing of sight and sound the film places viewers in the position of the common barnyard animals near the end of *Animal Farm* who sneak a peek into the dinner shared by the farmers and the ruling pigs and discover that it has become difficult to distinguish the pigs from the people.

The sound of I. F. Stone's uncluttered truth is often placed in opposition to the on-camera lies of a Johnson, Nixon, or McNamara. Stone printed the truth about the Tonkin Gulf incident only days after it happened, whereas the rest of the press simply repeated government statements. Because Stone was rejected by official Washington, he had to dig out his facts from under the avalanche of government documents and newspaper reports that were available to any reporter with two eyes and an open mind.

Stone is no wild-eyed radical; his appearance is more that of an anti-hero and his rhetoric delivered more with a passion for truth than a hatred for liars. He is living testimony that one person with limited resources can be important to a nation.

The film was made by Jerry Bruck over a three-year period in a *cinema verité* style that often has a home-made look. He nevertheless managed to take a visually unexciting subject and produce an important and engrossing documentary.

62 minutes, black and white, made from 1970 to 1973. From Open Circle Cinema.

Imprint

This French animation by artist Jacques Cardon is a Kafkaian tale of a society in which the children have a mold fastened to their backs with a giant key attached. Turning the key is part of mothering in this society, as is removing the mold at maturity. When the children are finally freed from the burden of the key and mold, they are left with a large and deep footprint in the back of the head.

Having reached the "age of freedom," a boy is taken by his mother to a huge door. The boy automatically crawls toward the door, which swings open to reveal hundreds of boys like himself, each stretched out on the ground with a man holding down his head with a booted foot.

Imprint can be viewed as simply another of the many pessimistic views of human nature so common to European film animation, or it can be seen as a hard but realistic view of the process of socialization and enculturation. In every society, parents imprint the young with certain values and place on their backs the burden of cultural beliefs and traditions. Many, or most, never overcome this early conditioning. It is Cardon's decision to view this imprinting as the establishing of a master/slave relationship. Cardon is very possibly condemning a certain kind of class society or possibly a certain kind of parenting or education that leaves youngsters with little choice but to follow quietly in the mold so carefully shaped for them from the date of birth.

Imprint employs stark but nicely executed drawings to present its case. The film is general enough to provoke a variety of thoughts, yet not too obscure to discourage interpretation. Any interpretation is bound to say more about the interpreter's own ideas of growing up than about the film itself.

7 minutes, color, animation, directed by Jacques Cardon (1975). From New Yorker Films.

The Incident

Quote from a 1974 news item in the *Arizona Daily Star:* "A jeering crowd in Dania, Florida, shouted to a twenty-seven-year-old woman to jump from a 110 foot tower which she had climbed in an apparent suicide attempt. The crowd pelted police with rocks as they tried to talk her down and booed them when they managed to bring her down. The police had to disperse the crowd. Five policemen received minor injuries before the woman was finally led away to safety."

The above incident is not too far removed from the fictional events depicted in the Polish animated film, *The Incident*. A pathetic everyman stands atop a skyscraper and prepares to jump. The ambulance sirens advertise the personal tragedy, which quickly becomes public entertainment. A crowd gathers and all the peddlers of cheap thrills converge on the scene—the reporters with their TV cameras and tape recorders, the ticket hawkers and food vendors, the owner of a telescope who charges for a better look, and even pickpockets.

But the man changes his mind about jumping and disappoints the crowd by descending in the elevator. The crowd has gathered for a show and finally takes drastic action to make sure that they have a tragedy to witness.

The Incident is a commentary on crowd psychology, social numbness in the face of real violence, and the psychological influence of television.

7 minutes, color, animated, directed by Bronislaw Zeman (1971). From Phoenix Films; rental also from Viewfinders.

In Continuo

In Continuo is a Yugoslavian film by Vlatko Gilic very much in the mood and style of his *One Day More.* Here the people are all men working in some unidentified, drab room. One scrubs what looks like rust stains from a white tile wall. Are these prisoners on a cleaning detail? Another drags chains, and viewers' minds leap to thoughts of concentration camps and some kind of terrible torture. One of the men is hoisted up crucifix-style on a hook and let down again—just testing. Eventually they sharpen long knives in a cacophony of rasping steel. With the sound of an erupting volcano, blood gushes through the room, and another ordinary workday in the slaughterhouse has begun.

But there are no victims, no animals, shown, only the blood. The blood flows in rivers and finally leaves the building to create its own stream outside, tainting the earth. *In Continuo* focuses so powerfully on the surface reality of preparing for a workday in a slaughterhouse that it arouses deeper fears and suggests more universal realities. An excellent, if gory, film.

12 minutes, color. From Phoenix Films; rental also from Viewfinders.

Interviews with My Lai Veterans

Interviews with My Lai Veterans, by Joseph Strick, won a recent Academy Award for the best short subject. The short was filmed by Richard Pearce and Haskell Wexler, the latter the cinematographer of *Who's Afraid of Virginia Woolf* and director of *Medium Cool.* Wexler once turned down Mike Nichols's offer to film *The Graduate* on the grounds that it was "irrelevant."

Interviews is far from irrelevant. The 20-minute film contains interviews with five My Lai veterans and makes for powerful viewing despite its lack of visual content other than talking faces. The normal, matter-of-fact behavior of the five contrasts sharply with their stories. The facts which emerge are that a search-and-destroy operation had been ordered that resulted in the destruction of a village and its inhabitants. According to the soldiers, about 450 people were killed by about 95 Americans. Three of the participants admit that they had taken part in the massacre, but none defends the action. They are all hesitant about discussing the less-publicized rape, mutilation, and scalping which also apparently took place.

20 minutes, color. From Macmillan Films; rental also from University of Michigan and University of California.

The Invention of the Adolescent

True or false: There really weren't any adolescents in the sixteenth century; adolescence is an invention of the eighteenth century and the Industrial Revolution. Moreover, it's not so much that teenagers drop out of society as that adults push them out by defining them as socially irrelevant. Finally, the real purpose for compulsory education is to keep kids off the streets and out of the factories.

These are the ideas explored in a National Film Board of Canada production appropriately titled *The Invention of the Adolescent.* The film points out that children used to pass from childhood right into adulthood. They were in contact with many adults during the day; they saw and helped with their fathers' work; they were a part of the birth, death, and sex of the family. What we today know as adolescence was created by the loss of contact with many adults through segregation in schools, the separation of the place of work from the home brought about by the factory system, the hiding of birth and death by social taboos, and the desire to preserve what is childlike through children's toys, literature, and emphasis on play.

Three centuries ago, high school age "children" would have been married and working. Today they are busy having problems adjusting and find themselves almost forced to create a subculture which adults are then forced to reject. School helps prevent "children" from growing up and hence adults from being ready to accept them.

The Invention of the Adolescent is a provocative film that probes the generation gap and the "youth problem" on a deeper level than most other films on the subject.

25 minutes, black and white. From NFBC; rental also from University of Michigan.

Invisible Walls

Invisible Walls is about the walls eighteen inches from our bodies in which we Americans mentally encase ourselves. The space inside of this invisible shield we unconsciously guard as personal. The film records how pedestrians were stopped for interviews only to have their "personal space" violated. Strangers who invade this 18 inches of personal space are told in body language to back off or that their closeness is considered an attack. Such behavior is learned, the narrator points out, and differs from culture to culture. Americans are physically aloof compared to other peoples who also live in crowded cities. American children accept contact as a part of life but soon learn to restrict touching others by a highly limited set of conditions. The film concludes that with increases in city size we either have to learn to tolerate more invasions of our personal space or learn to enjoy physical closeness. The film is excellent for discussion and a fine introduction to body language.

12 minutes, black and white. From University of California; rental also from University of Michigan.

The Island

This is another in the series of literature adaptations in Learning Corporation of America's "Classics, Dark and Dangerous" series. "The Island" is a short story by the British writer L. P. Hartley (1895—1972), who is best known to American audiences for his novels *The Go-Between* and *The Hireling*, both of which were made into feature films. How "classic" his short story is can be debated, but it is a good example of the British suspense-story genre.

The Island is a sinister tale of infidelity and revenge existing in what seems to be a moral vacuum. The protagonist, Simmonds, is a young British officer who is having an affair with a woman who lives in a lavishly appointed mansion on an otherwise seemingly deserted island. He has written ahead to say that he will spend his one day of leave with her. Arriving on the nearly inaccessible island, he is told by the very British butler that Mrs. Santander will join him later for dinner. The butler (who, of course, is suspicious because of his occupation) insists that Simmonds bathe and dress for dinner. While he is bathing, his pistol is secretly "borrowed" and then replaced.

Wandering around the mansion, Simmonds comes across a man who claims to be an electrician. But the "electrician" is later revealed as the husband of Simmonds's lover. Simmonds has walked into a trap and falls victim to the revenge of the jealous husband.

Exactly what happens we will leave for you to find out upon viewing the film. Suffice it to say that *The Island* is a well-produced thriller with a number of intriguing discussion possibilities. The film guide that accompanies it offers some interesting topics to explore.

30 minutes, color (1976). From LCA.

Island of Dreams: A Fable for Our Time

Island of Dreams is a Silvo Severi animation with an easily accessible yet almost universal message.

Using comic strip style art, Severi shows a man going through the rat race called "Earning a Living," fighting both people and traffic. After a humdrum eight hours, he returns home only to find no escape from noise and distraction. Naturally, he dreams of an island paradise, and thanks to poetic license he is transported to the island of his dreams.

The island retreat is truly a paradise with little for him to do but enjoy nature. Of course, he needs to construct shelter for protection against falling coconuts. He also needs an automatic stove for a fire, a generator for lights, and an auto for transportation. After a while our dreamer lives in a world little different from the one he was trying to escape. His island has become noisy and machinery-ridden.

An excellent film in the light of the current interest in back-to-nature and simpler life-styles.

10 minutes, animation. From Texture Films.

☐ ☐ ☐ ☐ ☐ ☐ ☐ ☐ ☐ ☐ ☐ ☐ ☐ ☐

J J J J J J J J J J J

☐ ☐ ☐ ☐ ☐ ☐ ☐ ☐ ☐ ☐ ☐ ☐ ☐

Joseph Schultz

Joseph Schultz is part of a superb film trilogy that includes *Silences* and *Death of a Peasant*. All three are highly professional films set in World War II Yugoslavia, and all deal with moral values tested at their raw extremities.

Joseph Schultz is based on the true story of a soldier who refused to serve in a firing squad to execute a row of nearly 20 peasants. The film gives no motivation for his refusal and no hint of why he lowers his gun and joins those to be executed. He is killed by his fellow soldiers.

The decision Schultz makes is extreme because war forces extremes and tests limits. But the same kind of value decisions are faced daily by civilians in less dramatic forms. *Joseph Schultz* can help to explore the forces at work undermining values and ultimately civilization itself. The film is easy to discuss, but the soldier's decision is difficult to comprehend.

13 minutes, color. From Wombat Productions; rental also from University of California and University of Michigan.

Joyce at 34

Joyce at 34 is a film by and about women that happily manages to avoid the feminist overkill that so often puts even an open-minded audience on the defensive. It is an honest presentation of the problems and joys of mixing motherhood, liberation, and child rearing. Joyce Chopra is the subject of the film as well as its co-director. We see her first daughter born in a beautiful natural childbirth scene, her coping with the added task of mothering while still working as a filmmaker, the problems with sharing child raising with her freelance writer husband, and the reaction of her parents to the child.

The film's honesty is disarming even to an audience hostile to "feminism." Joyce is an attractive role model for teenage girls, and her husband a challenge to adolescent boys. *Joyce at 34* is a well-made, enjoyable film for a study of marriage, parenting, women, or alternative life-styles. The film is also effective as a discussion provoker for adult audiences.

28 minutes, color (1973). From New Day.

Just Lather, That's All

A barber shop in an unnamed South American country provides the setting for a confrontation between a soldier who has come to town to round up and kill the local rebels and a barber who is himself a rebel. During his shave, the soldier brags of his imaginative torture of the enemy: "Too bad the whole town didn't see them—to see how miserable these revolutionaries are." The rebel barber presses the razor to the defenseless soldier's throat; only a flick of the wrist and a turn of conscience separate the latter from ignominious death.

The central image of metal against flesh is used to build tension and rivet viewers to every facial expression and every word of the ensuing dialogue. But *Just Lather, That's All* is no blood-and-guts, Kojak-in-the barbershop thriller. Instead, it closely follows the short story by Hernando Tellez from which it derives as it develops the theme of conscience and motivation. The soldier explains, "They call me a murderer, some people; but we all have to do what we have to do. We cannot change that; murderer, hero, it's all the same."

Rounding up rebels keeps the soldier in business just as giving shaves keeps the barber alive. Both long ago made the decisions about killing and being killed that shape their actions in this confrontation. The soldier not only knows the barber's mind, he is also aware of his other life as a rebel informer and has deliberately come to torture his conscience. In one sentence, he states the theme of the film and the source of his confidence: "No one deserves the sacrifice of having someone become a murderer." The barber knows that the soldier is right and will not allow this boasting professional killer to drag him down to a lower moral plane. When the shave is finished, the soldier straps on his gun and leaves, explaining, "They told me you would kill me, that you were a rebel. But killing is not easy, you can take my word for it."

Students who have grown up with typical TV violence believe that killing is as easy as pulling a trigger; this film questions that belief and proposes far deeper considerations. In spite of its lack of cinematic attractions, the story (which can be found in the paperback, *Contemporary Latin American Short Stories*, from Fawcett, 1974) has been well adapted to the screen by John Sebert. The film can be useful in literature courses.

21 minutes, color, directed by John Sebert. From LCA.

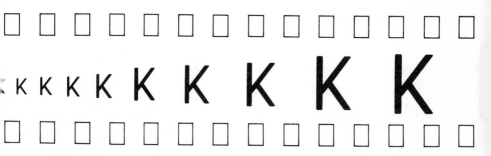

Kent State, May 1970

This film is an accurate visual case study of the events at Kent State University that led up to and include the actual shootings. Using still photographs, soundtrack, and the testimony of witnesses, its makers have faithfully reconstructed exactly what happened at Kent State. Director Al Cox was determined to make the film objective and yet was committed to showing that "gross injustice had been committed and was going not only unpunished but uninvestigated by a competent grand jury. It was our conviction that an objective presentation of the facts could convince people of the truth and of our point of view."

Remarkably, Cox was correct. The film was used in the legal investigation and finally was shown to the Federal Grand Jury so that the testimony of individual guardsmen could be matched against its visual documentation. Since that time, however, the indictments of the guardsmen have been dismissed.

E. G. Marshall narrates the film while standing at key places on the Kent State campus. The film makes clear that the presence of the Guard on campus as a sort of occupation army quickly overshadowed the issue of Cambodia as the students' cause of grievance. The doomed rally was a peaceful and legal attempt to seek redress for grievances, but when the commander of the National Guard ordered the students to disperse and they failed to do so, the troopers were ordered into action. Unknown to the students, the Guards' rifles were loaded with live ammunition. What happened next is part of the tragic side of American history.

Included in the documentary is super-8 footage taken by a student from a nearby tower. The visual action of the footage is incredibly similar to the massacre on the Odessa Steps, a sequence from Sergei Eisenstein's classic film, *Battleship Potemkin*.

Kent State, May 1970 is provocative both in its objectivity and the final argument by the narrator on the Guard's indefensible action. Authorities at Kent State ignored the dictates of justice and compassion in favor of keeping control and maintaining the status quo.

23 minutes, color, with excellent study guide (1972). From McGraw-Hill Films.

Krasner, Norman—Beloved Husband of Irma

This film is a satire on the pay-as-you-go toilet. After borrowing a dime to get into a pay toilet, our hero is further humbled by various technological idiosyncrasies such as a flooding toilet and a lack of toilet paper. The latter problem is solved with a recently purchased $19.95 coffee-table art book. For its ultimate insult, the toilet stall locks him in. Good humor springs from the most ordinary and universal of experiences. *Krasner, Norman—Beloved Husband of Irma* certainly gets a lot of mileage from a dime. A nice companion to 1501—1/2.

7 minutes, black and white. From CFS; rental also from Viewfinders.

Kurt Vonnegut, Jr.: A Self-Portrait

Writing is a "marvelous practical joke," according to one of the art's leading practitioners. Kurt Vonnegut, Jr., laughs almost to tears when he tells of the "joke" of writing. As a writer, he says, "I can make marks on paper that will cause someone far away to cry; the damn fool will actually cry." He marvels at writing as a way for a poor man to circulate ideas; a sheet of paper still costs less than a penny.

During the depression, Vonnegut's father was an unemployed architect. His mother wrote short stories for extra income. At high school in Indianapolis, he wrote for one of the nation's few daily school papers. He claims that because of this learning opportunity the school has produced "lots of writers." His own influences came from reading whatever was in the family library—"a literary smorgasbord." During these early years he was also influenced by comedians like Laurel and Hardy and Jack Benny; "they expressed genius of a high order; they sustained people during the depression."

But Vonnegut's formal training was more as a scientist than as writer; he studied more chemistry in school than fiction. This scientific background (he worked briefly as a public relations writer for General Electric) has led him to a combination of writing and science—science fiction. Indeed, his stories have always been generated by asking fascinating "what if" questions and answering them in a story.

So far this review has said a bit about Vonnegut, but nothing about the film. But that is how Harold Mantell directed his portrait of Vonnegut; the viewer has a chance to meet Vonnegut as a person rather than as a celebrity. Film technique never intrudes or interferes with the presentation of this delightfully entertaining, witty, and only slightly eccentric writer. Even viewers who have never read Vonnegut might want to consider doing so after screening *Kurt Vonnegut, Jr.: A Self-Portrait.*

29 minutes, color, directed by Harold Mantell (1976). From Films for the Humanities.

Last Hour Clash: Part of the Heart of Teaching

Discipline problems are the bane of many a teacher's existence. Pythagoras kept dropping triangles in the back of the class, Eddie Cummings defiantly refused to use capital letters, and Al Einstein kept turning in the same funny looking equation for every homework assignment. Every teacher has at least one student who appears in nightmares. For junior high school science teacher, Whit Jefferson, the nightmare is named Sydney.

Sydney is no knife-wielding punk, just your typical discipline problem, but he drives Whit to primal screaming on his way home. Whit calls a parents conference and the dad complains, "If the kid acts up at home, do we come crying to you?" All Whit's efforts to control Sydney meet with failure. Finally, a conference with Sydney and the willingness to compromise lead to the discovery that Sydney cannot understand the subject matter. Whit sets up a special after-school class and lives happily ever after. The film is not designed to show a method for dealing with every Sydney. It is intended to help a group of teachers share ways of coping with frustration.

Last Hour Clash is an excellent, humorous film for teachers to use in professional improvement courses. Judging from this one film, the entire "The Heart of Teaching" series of five films would make a productive course in teacher training or continuing education. Other films in the series are The Parent Crunch (about encounters with angry parents), An Eye for Change (the risks and worries of professional growth), Every One Is Something Else (recognizing individual differences), and A Faculty Feeling (isolation and loneliness).

15 minutes, color. Sale only from AIT.

Last Stand Farmer

People used to have less, but they also had fewer needs and were happier. Such is the view of progress of Kenneth O'Donnell, a 67-year-old Vermont farmer whose only concessions to the twentieth century are a TV and a chain saw. It's not that O'Donnell hasn't tried modern methods of farming. He bought a tractor once but never drove it: "I still like my horses—to hell with the tractor."

O'Donnell is being forced off his farm. There is freedom of speech in Vermont and other Constitutional freedoms, but evidently little freedom to be an inefficient, anachronistic farmer. His taxes doubled in one year, and the only way to pay them was to sell some of the 180-acre farm. Land in Vermont is assessed at market value, and the market reflects the values of land developers rather than stubborn, eccentric old farmers. O'Donnell is an independent, and his days are numbered even without considering his age.

There have been many documentaries about the forces pushing farmers off the land and about the tendency of agriculture to be replaced by agri-business, but *Last Stand Farmer* deals only in specifics and never in the generalities that characterize other documentaries. Director Richard Brick became a friend of O'Donnell and made *Last Stand Farmer* out of respect for the man and his integrity. The photography is simple and plain as the life-style it presents. As the film ends, O'Donnell tends to his two draft horses on a winter day. "Some people wouldn't give a nickel for this place in winter. But after you've lived on it for a lifetime, it's the only place you'd want to be." The film has received ten major film awards, including the John Grierson Award of the 1976 American Film Festival.

28 minutes, color, directed by Richard Brick (1975). From Silo Cinema.

The Late Show

The camera slowly pans around a room, spotting a family picture, cardboard boxes, open cereal, a dented *Colt 45* beer can. On television John Wayne in *Red River* has again emerged victorious and is followed by a procession of late night commercials. U.S. Steel proclaims itself the builder of the launching pad that helped put "the free world into orbit"; Pepsi declares itself as "the taste that comes on big." The camera continues its motion and finally discovers the occupant of the room—a black man watching TV, drinking beer, and carefully cleaning his rifle. The commercials continue: GE announces its "most important kind of progress" and Pepsi now tries the girl-watching approach: "Try it, someone will be watching." After this final disgorge of ads, the station goes through its sign-off ritual playing the National Anthem: "Perilous strife, bombs bursting in air." The camera stops on the man's face, half dark and half light. "Land of the free, home of the brave." The screen goes blank.

The Late Show uses juxtaposition with great economy, giving each sound and image multiple meanings. The John Wayne film is used as ironic counterpoint, as in Peter Bogdanovich's *The Last*

Picture Show. Each TV image is familiar, yet in the context of the black man with a gun they take on undertones of hypocrisy, fear, and absurdity. The images speak of violence, the John Wayne mystique, the Wild West, progress, white ideals, acceptance, man on the moon, the free world, and "ring around the collar."

The film will provoke an audience in terms of its own prejudices. How many viewers, influenced by TV news, will assume that the black is a black militant? *The Late Show* is aptly named; it is not so much about race as it is about television as a shaper of values and of what we perceive as reality.

12 minutes, black and white (1972). From Films Inc.; rental also from Viewfinders.

Learning to Live

Learning to Live is an eight-part television series produced by the Methodist Church and now available in 16mm. The series presents the ideas of Transactional Analysis (à la Eric Berne and Thomas Harris) in a group discussion format. The group leader, Stephen Winners, conducts a low-key discussion with about a dozen adults. Two or three film clips applying TA to real life are used in the course of each program.

The discussion is excellent, and the viewer becomes a silent participant in the group. Winners's examples strike home, and most

viewers will find themselves saying "that's me" more than once during each film.

I previewed the film on *Feelings* (No. 5 in the series) and found it a fascinating exploration of how people "save up" feelings only to take them out later on some innocent bystander. Winners makes the key observation that we often get into the position of considering our feelings "magical." That is, they are viewed as being like the weather—states of being that *happen to us* rather than human experiences that are subject to our control. His approach is to emphasize that no one can make you think, feel, act, or believe in any way you don't choose, that you are responsible for your own feelings.

Other titles include *Ego States, Transactions, Strokes, Time Structures, Games, Acquiring Life Scripts*, and *Changing Life Scripts*.

29 minutes each, color. From MMM.

Leisure

An animated film that presents novel ideas about the state of society today is rare. A film commissioned by a government agency that is both entertaining and enlightening is even rarer. So to discover an animated film commissioned by a department of the Australian Government that creatively and perceptively deals with the growing problem of the "art of leisure" is a pleasant surprise. Add to these surprises a 1977 Academy Award for best animated film, and *Leisure* becomes a "must see."

Leisure is animated by Bruce Petty, an artist best known for his political cartoons, which have appeared in *New Yorker* and *Punch*. His cartoon style lends itself nicely to the understated humor-with-insight of the script. What makes *Leisure* such an exceptional film is the ability of the narration to present new, even startling, ideas and to make viewers question their own concept of what is "work" and what is "play."

The film begins by tracing a brief history of leisure. Industry made the chaotic world of the primitive more orderly and thus divided society into two groups—one that did all the getting, overcoming, and solving that became known as "work," and another that did all the sitting, playing, and dreaming that came to be known as "leisure." This division of effort lasted for thousands of years until the discovery of equality and the profit margin. It was decided that everyone could have some leisure but that it must be separated from work. "Electricity and optimism were everywhere, and it seemed only a matter of time before everybody owned one of everything and was content." But segmentation was the serpent in the garden of leisure, and "it was thought the human mind may have lost the art of leisure."

Then dawned today's age of self-expression, but "everybody expressing themselves simultaneously was causing tension and [high] blood pressure."

Now the film moves from history to prophecy, and planners see that much urban space could be used for two functions. Parking lots and factory grounds could double as markets or running tracks, rooftops could be gardens, movie screens could be suspended buildings. Human beings now realize that leisure must be planned as carefully as work—daylight saving, dawn work, the siesta, staggered workday, flexible workweek, winter work year, split-work lifetime.

"A new thought occurred. It could be that instead of work being what people wanted with enough leisure to make it bearable, it might be that leisure was what people wanted with enough work to make it possible. But instead of industry deciding the times and spaces for leisure, leisure should be deciding the times and spaces for industry. That instead of growth rate, a satisfaction rate should be the human measure."

Leisure is one of the most thought-provoking animated films to come along in quite a while. Find some time to view it—if you're not too busy working, that is.

14 minutes, color, animated, directed by Bruce Petty (1976). From Pyramid Films; rental also from Viewfinders.

Lovejoy's Nuclear War

On the anniversary of George Washington's Birthday, 1974, Samuel Holden Lovejoy, a farmer, toppled a 500-foot steel tower in Montague, Massachusetts. The tower had been erected by the local utility as part of its project to construct a multimegawatt, multibillion dollar, twin nuclear power plant on the Montague Plains.

Leaving 350 feet of twisted wreckage behind him, Lovejoy hitched a ride to the police station where he turned himself in and submitted a four-page written statement decrying the dangers of nuclear power and declaring his act one of self-defense. His act of sabotage acted as a catalyst for the local community, both energizing and alienating, but demanding a stand. Before his act of civil disobedience, people in Montague more or less accepted the nuke as something wise men had decided necessary.

Lovejoy's Nuclear War is a timely film that goes far beyond the desirability of nuclear power plants in subject matter. Basically, the film is about the value of, or need for, civil disobedience in the face of seemingly unstoppable technology. As Lovejoy comments at his trial, "The environment must be protected, and life must be protected, and somehow we've got to be able to confront this all-pervading technology that's beginning to drown us with some counterbalance."

Much of the film consists of interviews with Lovejoy, nuclear scientist John Gofman, Charles Bragg of the public relations department at Northeast Utilities, residents of Montague, and Howard Zinn, a political science professor who advocates civil disobedience in times of grave danger. Scientist Gofman is very much opposed to nuclear plants on the basis that with a nuclear plant "you've created an astronomical amount of radioactive garbage, which you must contain and isolate better than 99.99 percent perfectly. . . . Do you believe there's anything you'd like to guarantee will be done 99.99 percent perfectly for a hundred thousand years?"

Charles Bragg, of the Northeast Utilities, considers the opposition simply antiscience. "They'd be as much against an electric toothbrush, if you will, as they would be against nuclear power plants. It's a life-style with them. You have to weigh that against the great body of scientific knowledge and western civilization, which pretty much has put an imprimatur on nuclear power." He compares building nuclear power plants to building railways in the 1840s, saying that "there would be no railroads built if one or a group of towns could block the line."

Both Presidents Nixon and Ford called for the construction of 200 major nuclear power plants within ten years as part of Project Independence. Plans call for 1000 reactors operating in America by the end of the century. Meanwhile, more and more citizens are learning of the dangers involved in the storage of radioactive wastes for periods of up to 200,000 years, the possibility of a catastrophic "melt down," the threat of sabotage, thermal pollution, and the long-term effects of low-level radiation. The switch to nuclear energy might be a life-saving scientific advance or a corporate con job with utterly unacceptable risks. Sam Lovejoy helps force viewers to make a commitment on the question.

Technically, the film is good with only a few lapses in contrast and sound. The subject matter is timely, important, and provocatively presented.

Does Sam Lovejoy still sit in jail serving time for "willful and malicious destruction of personal property"? Was he able to win the jury over to his viewpoint? You'll have to see the film to find out.

60 minutes, color, directed by Dan Keller (1975). From Green Mountain Post Films; rental also from University of California.

Machine

Machine is a 10-minute animation item from the Janus New Cinema collection, now available from Pyramid. In a world of black humor and absurdity, an angelically inspired man invents a machine. The machine provides clothes for the ordinary mortals who live on the lower levels of a universe that resembles a Picasso skyscraper. The inventor proceeds to build a bigger machine, one with a huge mechanical hand. After the hand dispatches a competitor below who is making his own machine, it provides houses for the people, who have at last discovered marriage. The new marriages produce babies, and the inventor-machine responds with beach balls. The babies have a disturbing tendency to grow up and increase the population. So the machine is again improved and now produces cannon, which the men below applaud and obediently use to keep down their number. The considerate machine plays the organ and sounds the church bells at the funeral of the war dead and even turns out coffins. The corpses applaud.

Finally after more inventions, each greeted with jubilation, the machine decides to take over. It easily eliminates its creator and takes over as king. Until the final scene that is. A cage slips over the machine, and a huge hook from the sky carries it upward. So it goes.

10 minutes, color, animated. From Pyramid Films; rental also from University of California.

Magic Machines

When we adults put aside the things of childhood, we make a mistake; we have snuffed out part of our humanity. But that is the price we are willing to pay for the mixed blessings of maturity. Julian Huxley said that to call a person "mature" is something of an insult. I think Mr. Huxley would enjoy *Magic Machines.* So will most viewers.

Robert Gilbert is a 25-year-old sculptor who takes what society labels junk and turns it into magic machines that bring fantasy to life. "I like fantasy, it's realer than most of the reality. . . . I'm a child, I never grew up. . . . I'm not planning on growing up."

Gilbert's kinetic sculptures are toys as well as social commentary. The "Knight of Fantasy" questions the division between reality and unreality, the "Rape of the Flower" confronts the values of technological "progress," and "June 23" portrays police brutality.

Gilbert narrates the film, and his works are allowed to speak for themselves through imaginative cinematography. For a film about a social dropout who considers himself a "freak, a victim of our society" to win an Academy Award, you know it must be good. Use the film to discuss art, social values, alternate life-styles, growing up, or maybe magic. As the film says: "There is this magic show. Some people are the magic show. Some people wonder what magic is and others know."

14 minutes, color. From LCA; rental also from University of Michigan.

The Man and the Snake

The snake has been an ambiguous symbol throughout history, embodying both all that is evil and the ultimate in curative powers. The mere word "snake" sends tremors of fear through many; imagine yelling "snake" instead of "fire" in a crowded theater.

In *The Man and the Snake*, based loosely on an Ambrose Bierce short story, both Bierce and filmmaker Sture Rydman twist the emotions of the audience from humor to courage to downright terror. *The Man and the Snake* is more frightening than many feature films because its object of fear is a real creature, one that might be lurking out in the backyard this very moment and one far more likely to be encountered than a hairy gorilla or garish visitor from the outer galaxies.

The Man and the Snake is a bit of self-torture for any viewer who allows the filmmaker to send chills up his spine and plant the seeds of future nightmares. The story takes place in Victorian England in the household of a Dr. Druring, a zoologist with a collection of snakes in his conservatory, which he jokingly calls "the snakery." The tutor joins the family for dinner, where he hears a story of a boa constrictor that placed a man under its spell in order to victimize him. The tutor, Harker Brayton, rejects the story as nonsense. He decides to spend the night and falls asleep reading about snakes. Suddenly, he awakes to see two beady eyes on the floor near his bed; the eyes draw him to them hypnotically as the snake crawls closer and closer. The eyes loom ever larger until. . . . Well, why spoil a good horror film?.

The Man and the Snake is a well-constructed film, useful in teaching about the adaptation of short stories to film, about snakes as a symbol, about the genre of the horror story, about the construction of suspense, about the works of Ambrose Bierce, or simply as masochistic entertainment.

26 minutes, color, made in 1972, released in 1976. From Pyramid Films.

Marceau on Mime

Marceau on Mime is a beautiful presentation of a man eloquent both in the art of mime and that of expressive speaking. In this informal talk, interspersed with line drawings and photos, Marceau expounds on the theory and philosophy of mime as an art form. It is a universal language thousands of years old, which has been kept alive by modern masters such as Pierrot, Chaplin, Keaton, and even Laurel and Hardy.

Marceau practices mime as the art of metamorphosis, a discipline akin to zen or yoga meditation. To be a mime, Marceau explains, is to be able to identify with all the elements that surround us. The mimer is enveloped by an invisible world he magically makes visible. In mime, the concrete is made abstract and the abstract concrete. What a painter draws on canvas, the mimer draws in space.

Marceau has a powerful yet warm and engaging personality. Viewers hang on almost every word he speaks and cannot help leaving the film feeling that the art of mime is a wondrous world to explore.

The film's only weakness is the absence of Marceau performing his art. But that is perhaps best saved for another day.

22 minutes, color. From Paramount Films.

Martin the Cobbler

Leo Tolstoy was a deeply religious man, but on his own terms. He saw much of religion as pernicious superstition and often wrote of gov-

ernment, slavery, and religion in the same terms. He described a "terrible" superstition as "one similar in every respect to religious superstition. It consists in the affirmation that, besides the duties of man to man, there are still more important obligations to an imaginary being. In theology, the imaginary being is God, and in political science the imaginary being is Government." His religion was human-centered, and this animated adaptation of his short story, "Where Love Is, God Is," should be viewed with that in mind.

Martin was a poor cobbler who had lost his family and his desire to live. In a dream, he hears the Lord's voice promising to visit him the next day. Instead, poor people in need of food, clothing, and warmth come to Martin's door, and he helps them. He changes from a cynical and desolate old man to a warm, loving, and vital person. He finds meaning in helping others in need.

Martin the Cobbler balances on the edge of simple-mindedness ("this is a film that teaches you to be nice to people—even to rats"), but it can also be a pure and simple reminder about service to people in need.

The superb clay animation by Will Vinton (who also did *Closed Mondays* and *Mountain Music*) is a joy to watch. Production values are excellent all around.

28 minutes, color, animation, directed by Will Vinton (1977). From Billy Budd Films; rental also from MMM.

Meditation

Meditation is an audience-participation film, a primer in the art of meditating. Alan Watts conducts the introductory lesson in meditation, which he describes as "getting in touch with reality, the art of temporarily silencing the mind." Western man thinks of meditation in terms of occupying the mind with thoughts, but the Eastern expert knows that a person who thinks all the time has nothing to think about except thoughts—mere chattering inside the skull. The mind cannot be forced into silence; imagine trying to force yourself not to think of an elephant for two minutes. In order to demonstrate how silence of mind is achieved, Watts leads viewers through several experiments.

"Hear all that's around you," he instructs. "Don't try to identify sounds. Listen without asking what it means. Be concerned with what is—not past or future, only now. Don't seek a result; simply be here in the world of sound and the eternal now."

He goes on to demonstrate how a gong and mantra can aid meditation and leads the audience in an OM chant. He describes "OM" as an audio rainbow encompassing the entire range of sound. He gives lessons on breathing techniques and the proper posture for meditation. He allots a quiet time in the film for a bit of practice in meditation. But the film unexpectedly ends with a different kind of meditation when the viewer is advised to "put your hands on your hips and just laugh."

An excellent film for a cooperative audience willing to take the lesson seriously. Watts's instruction will hardly lead to the instant creation of meditation experts, but they will give insight into the difference between Eastern and Western approaches to reality.

28 minutes, color. From the directors and producers, Harlety Productions.

Men's Lives

Growing up male in America is just as problematic as growing up female. One of the main differences between the two sets of problems is that women realized the difficulty first and now have help from one another in gaining liberation or equilibrium. Males once spoke of the "woman problem" in much the same way that whites used to speak of the "black problem." Now males are beginning to realize that the social definition of maleness is itself a problem. *Men's Lives* is the first quality documentary to deal with the problem of growing up male in America.

Will Roberts and Josh Hanig are filmmakers in their mid-twenties who set out to document their own passage to masculinity and relate that to the larger picture of men's lives. By speaking of their own experience and adeptly interviewing articulate men (but avoiding experts—psychologists, etc.) they have produced an excellent and highly useful film document.

Young boys like to boss others, a grade school teacher observes. They stand around on a playground and readily point out which ones are "sissies." A nearby girl admits she thinks it is harder to be a girl since boys get to do more. TV and movie clips illustrate the masculine image of the media from John Wayne to Mr. Universe. Boys learn early and begin to test their concept of masculinity.

An articulate teen who likes ballet and gymnastics admits he is still embarrassed about it, while a young black football player says he loves his sport because he "just likes to kill. You kill them or they kill you." A black teen dreams out loud about getting a "nice blue Cadillac," while his white counterpart drives a custom car and admits it makes him feel more masculine.

From the proving ground of adolescence, the film moves to a college party where conquering the opposite sex takes priority. Women become the most difficult test of masculinity, since it is not permissible to show insecurity in their company.

After college or the army, the concept of masculinity is used to shape a career. As one interviewer in the film observes: "Most men in this society see themselves as failures, and the reason is that there's always someone around the corner who has a nicer car, an extra room on their house—so they strive to be better than that person—only to find out that there's someone else with two cars, and both of them are nicer than theirs." A barber, who claims—somewhat startlingly— that "men open up and tell me as a barber many things they wouldn't tell their father-confessor," finds that most men lack a sense of satisfaction in their lives.

The interviews define the problem of masculinity with poignancy and surprising depth. The filmmakers attach a weak conclusion: Our society requires this kind of man. But the value of *Men's Lives* lies in its recognition of the problem of masculinity and in its ability to stimulate an audience to begin to deal with the problem on a personal and social level.

43 minutes, color (1974). From New Day Films.

Merc

Merc lives in Grand Central Station. The filmmaker noticed him "because he didn't move." He stands, arms at sides, for hours at a time. A couple of times a day he will walk across the station. He survives with money from telephone coin return boxes and sleeps on the window ledge of the Oyster Bar. Merc seems a modern-day

Bartleby, an anonymous and forgotten part of the scenery, no more deserving of attention than a floor tile in the train station.

The filmmaker approaches Merc cautiously after long days of observation. Merc's first words are "I type" and "I can't pick." The filmmaker becomes obsessed with finding out what kind of world Merc sees "out there." He contacts Merc and finally allows him to hold the camera as if that will reveal his world. The filmmaker becomes increasingly involved in Merc's strange life and finally takes him to his apartment.

Merc, as you may judge from the above description, is a curious documentary and that is how it "views." Only at the end credits do viewers realize that Merc is played by an actor and that the whole film is fiction. *Merc*, which has won a number of film festival awards, is truly a unique experience. Amos Vogel claims that *Merc* is a "mysterious, deceptive, and significant achievement [which] raises very serious philosophical questions about truth and illusion, art and reality, *cinema verité* and fiction, 'authenticity' in film and how to recognize it." I personally find *Merc* more "sneaky" than "philosophical," but I also find it so refreshingly different that it warrants a viewing by serious film students.

Merc functions on two levels: It is a story about a social reject and his world; it is also an examination of the cinematic relationship of the observer and the observed.

35 minutes, color, directed by Mark Obenhaus (1973). From Western World Productions.

Metamorphosis

Our unnamed hero is a "bookeeper type" who eats breakfast every morning out of a plastic cereal bowl, listens to the day's disasters on the morning news, descends in an elevator to the ground level of his high rise apartment, rides a bus to work, operates an adding machine all day, returns home, watches television, goes to bed, and starts the routine all over again. He is trapped with very little time to himself. Others, seeking an alternative lifestyle, might run off to a farm or the woods, but not our hero. He decides that the daily elevator ride can afford an opportunity to live "more deeply."

Over a period of months he practices so that he is able to do a little bit more on each elevator trip. He begins by trying to undress and then dress again before the doors open on the ground floor. This mastered, he moves on to bigger and better things like making coffee, reading the paper, shaving, smoking a cigarette, eating breakfast, and doing some take-home work. Thanks to the magic of film pixilation, he is able to lead a secret life compressed into the normally wasted time of an elevator ride.

Our frenzied hero has, in a sense, extended his life by creating more time—a dream shared in different ways by many people from Ponce de Leon to experimenters with cryonics to the clients of plastic surgeons. He has beaten the rat race; or so it seems at first. After less than a year of such high-speed living, he has become so proficient that he can compress an entire day's activities into the elevator ride and still have time left for a quick game of solitaire. But one morning the door opens on the ground floor to reveal the cost of cheating time—he has died an old man. Time has its revenge.

Filmmaker Barry Greenwald has chosen to use the descent in an elevator as an image for all of life. He seems to suggest that we must ultimately pay a price for an "instant society" in which "time is money" and "every minute counts." The cliché of urban life as "frantic and harried" is taken in *Metamorphosis* and given fresh life.

11 minutes, black and white, directed by Barry Greenwald at Conestoga College, Canada (1975). From CFS; rental also from Viewfinders.

Mind over Body

This film is a BBC documentary about psychosomatics and the human ability to make the expression "mind over matter" come true. On the Battleship New Jersey, an experiment (widely reported in the news media at the time) indicated that those sailors who had recently gone through "life changes" were those most likely to become ill. The experiment suggests that all illnesses have some element of the psychosomatic. In other words, germs and viruses of themselves do not completely explain why people get sick.

Other experiments are shown in which people are taught to control what had previously been considered involuntary bodily functions. In Canada a man learns to wiggle his ears by using videotape as a feedback mechanism. Senior Citizens in Boston come to a research center twice a week and learn to lower their blood pressure through visual feedback and small rewards. A younger man is taught to reduce his anxiety about the draft. Some viewers see frightening possibilities in this latter experiment, which has earmarks of *1984* attitude control.

Ramon Torres, a self-taught Peruvian, illustrates his ability to control pain by calmly pushing a bicycle spoke in one cheek and out the other. *Mind over Body* has an extensive section on alpha waves and meditation. Perhaps the most significant experiment shown takes place in Los Angeles where a young boy is taught to bring his long history of epileptic seizures under control.

The film's conclusions are cautious and in keeping with the tentative nature of the scientific results so far. *Mind over Body* is an

excellent documentary with fascinating visuals and narration. It is superb for the study of the human potential, the role of science, and the future of basic psychology.

50 minutes, color. From Time-Life Films.

More Than a School

This is a documentary about an alternative school within a school. Juniors and seniors in a Jewish, upper-class Long Island high school are offered the option of participating in a "community school." The viewpoint of the film is that the regular high school is big, bad, alienating, and disliked by students, while the community school is free, democratic, and utopian. All the interviews and scenes are selected to reinforce this dichotomy.

The community school, made up of 109 students and four teachers, uses local resources, allows students to help make decisions, offers a wide variety of courses, and manages to overcome student apathy. Some students teach courses, some work in the community as part of their education, and some even involve their parents in school activities.

Martha Coolidge's film successfully captures the exuberance and spirit of the community school and will make ideal showing for disgruntled teachers looking for a change or students who might want to participate in such a program. The film might also inspire others to experiment with change; if so, it will be worth the showing. But viewers would do well to avoid being swept up in the enthusiasm of the true believers.

The students (and teachers) who speak in the film offer an amazing number of clichés in supporting this form of learning. One law of communication is that the more likely and predictable a message, the less information it contains. Clichés in particular contain little information and are often a sign that those speaking have not yet asked the right questions or have answered them in only a superficial manner.

A valid question to ask about the experiment is: "Is this an example of the Hawthorne effect? Have conditions at the school become so bad that the most dissatisfied students would accept almost any alternative as a godsend simply because it is an alternative?" Any serious discussion of the film should deal with questions like this one, but ultimately the discussion must ask, "Is there anything in our school that could be improved by using some of the ideas from *More Than a School*"?

55 minutes, color. From Films Inc.

A Mother's Tale

What if cows suddenly gained self-awareness? What if one cow escaped the drive to the butcher and returned to the range to tell other cows that they are bred only to serve as victims? The message might be, "Each one of us is . . . alone, not of the herd. We are all betrayed, all who are put on the range. . . . We are brought into this life to be victims. Never be taken, never be driven; those who can do so, kill man. So long as man holds dominion over us, bear no young."

James Agee asked himself this "what if" question and discovered in it an apt allegory of human behavior. In *A Mother's Tale*, a mother cow relates to her offspring the story of a young bull who tried to warn the other cattle of their fate. But the offspring are skeptical of tales from a parent; they believe it an honor to go off on the huge trucks to some strange and exciting adventure. The mother's tale of a cow who had gained the knowledge of good and evil is not believed by the young. Even the mother admits that "it's just an old, old legend—we use it to frighten children." And so the slaughter continues, cows remain in their role as docile victims, and shoppers go on complaining of the high cost of rib steaks.

A Mother's Tale is not a children's story. It is a complex parable of the prophet who is without honor in his own country, of our unwillingness to accept the one message capable of granting our salvation. Every culture has its own version of the mother's tale, which it somehow knows is true, yet refuses to use as a basis for action. The story of Christ is often used as an old legend to frighten children into behaving. And what of the modern "seers" who prophesy ecological or population growth disaster unless we believe their tales of our fate? *A Mother's Tale* is a fascinating story for use with almost any age group.

Maureen Stapleton and Orson Welles do a fine job serving as the off-screen voices for the film. Filmmaker Rex Goff does only an adequate job of filming live action sequences of cattle to serve as a sort of minimal visual attraction. The story is so strong (once the audience accepts the plausibility of a talking cow) that the sometimes grainy pictorial effects have only to stay out of the way for the film to succeed.

The original Agee short story can be found in Bantam's *50 Great American Short Stories*. An interesting companion film would be *Imprint*.

18 minutes, color, directed by Rex Goff (1976). From LCA.

Moving Pictures: The Art of Jan Lenica

Jan Lenica (pronounced "len-sa") is a Polish animator and director of shorts such as *A, Labyrinth, Orfeo, Rhinoceros*, and a half-dozen others. His work is characterized by black humor, satire, and a generally dark view of existence. What is perhaps most impressive about Lenica's films is the creativity of their execution, and that is what director Richard Rogers has chosen to focus on in this film.

Lenica appears in a bare room, sitting before a desk with a microphone. The scene is appropriate more to a grilling followed by torture than to an interview with a filmmaker. But the setting captures the mood of Lenica's films perfectly and fits the anti-interview he grants.

Lenica explains that "I make films because I like it—sometimes they are fun and sometimes not. Every film is a part of me; in all my films it's always the same one man who wears different masks." But Lenica cannot give an engaging interview. As he admits, "I don't like to talk; I don't trust words."

And so the film concentrates on Lenica at his sketchboard and animation stand performing the lonely, painstaking task of creative animation. Excerpts from a number of his films are also shown.

Moving Pictures is not so much a film about animation or even about the ideas and techniques of Lenica himself as it is about the loneliness, dedication, and pain of the artist who chooses animation as a means of expression because "I don't trust words."

19 minutes, color, directed by Richard Rogers (1975). From Phoenix Films; rental also from Viewfinders.

The Murderer

In this adaptation of Ray Bradbury's short story, Albert Brock is a self-declared prophet struggling to lead the masses out of a technological wilderness. Brock is "The Murderer"; his victims are communication devices. He has been institutionalized for pouring French chocolate ice cream into his car radio, for dispatching his wrist radio, and for shooting his television set, "that obedient Medusa that turns people to stone every night."

To Brock, communication devices are the enemy, not because communication is evil, but because its instruments intrude on our lives and consume time and thought. Of the telephone, Brock philosophizes that it "drains away personality through wires. Only the cold fish of a voice is left. It just sits there and demands you call somebody. If not the telephone, it was TV, radio, movies, commercials, wrist radio-phones, interoffice communications, background music."

In Bradbury's original story (printed in the short story collection titled *The Golden Apples of the Sun*), Brock is interviewed by a psychiatrist, thus providing a dramatic excuse to expound his philosophy. In the film of *The Murderer*, the plot has been complicated to the point of confusion. Brock is played as a madman and the psychiatrist as an eccentric genius, who comes off more like a Richard Nixon trying to act in a high school play. There is a subplot involving the psychiatrist and his associates that remains unclear to me after a single viewing. The sets are duly futuristic, and the constant communication "noise" in the institution is appropriately irritating.

In spite of dramatic weaknesses, the message of Brock comes through clearly, although less so than in the original story. *The Murderer* is an excellent discussion vehicle for use with students who believe that the first step in starting a car is to turn on the radio, that a beach and a transistor radio are organic companions, and that silence is a curse.

28 minutes, color, directed by Andrew Silver. From Phoenix Films; rental also from Viewfinders.

Musereel

Musereel is a service of the nonprofit Centre for Internationalizing the Study of English. They have over three hours of film of poets reading their own work, and they will rent or sell it at truly nonprofit prices. The poets—from all over the world—include people like Louis Simpson, W.H. Auden, Allen Ginsberg, and Sir John Gielgud reading Noel Coward. The poets read well, and the films are an excellent way to present lively poetry.

The most unique aspect of *Musereel* is that the reading of any one poet or group of poets can be custom ordered by the minute, plus a lab fee. For more details write for a brochure from Michael Hazard, CIE/Media Central, 628 Grand Avenue, St. Paul, Minn. 55105.

My Goat

My Goat is about fantasy, children, warmth, and companionship in a mechanical society. A young boy is alone in his room in a high-rise apartment. He has an array of toys that reflect today's society—a plane, a robot, a moon walker. His toys are mechanical ones that ask a child only for a wind-up and then degrade him into being merely a spectator. The boy is bored and shows a streak of aggravation not far beneath the surface. To paraphrase Winston Churchill, "First we shape our toys; then our toys shape us."

To counter his mechanical and plastic world, the boy fantasizes having a baby goat as an imaginary companion. As the boy and the goat begin to play, some of the creativity and warmth missing earlier in the film emerge.

When the boy awakes the next morning, he finds the apartment that he and his goat left in shambles restored to order. He searches in vain for his companion until he opens the refrigerator door and finds that yesterday's fantasy has turned into tomorrow's roast. The boy throws off his pajamas and runs toward the camera in anguish.

My Goat is from the Dunav studios but does not measure up to their other productions. It resembles a student film, being decidedly flawed in both concept and execution. Even though the film does not "work"—the ending seems forced—it presents some attractive discussion possibilities.

15 minutes, color, directed by Mika Milosevic. From Wombat Productions.

□ □ □ □ □ □ □ □ □ □ □ □ □ □ □

N N N N N N N N N N

□ □ □ □ □ □ □ □ □ □ □ □ □ □

Natural Habitat

"If we were wide awake we would be instantly struck by the horrors which surround us. Could the man or woman who is so thoroughly awakened possibly do the crazy things which are now expected of him or her every moment of the day?" This is a quote from Henry Miller used to set the tone for *Natural Habitat*.

Ralph Arlyck's 1970 film is a nonnarrated look at the effects of dehumanized work environments. Beginning with a slow escalator descent of people, presumably into the hell of their daily jobs, the film shows the mass producers of doughnuts, the paper pushers and the paper picker-uppers, the builders, and the wreckers. Hard at work in the Schlitz factory is the man paid to watch beer bottles glide by on a conveyor belt. Bored at work are the disc jockey with the hip voice and the hip capitalist salesman promising liberation but selling only clothes.

Two recurring images in the film are those of a zoo and of a department store demonstration of Teflon cookware. The Teflon lady is a human wind-up doll who recites her prepared speech with all the passion of a vending machine. The zoo is compared visually to human society. Zoo animals are taken out of their natural habitats and placed in cages. The film suggests that many work roles place people in equally unnatural habitats. With animals and humans juxtaposed in this fashion, what emerges is a new kind of animal, one so adapted to an unnatural environment that he is far removed from the "natural" creature. Both the captive animals that zoogoers admire and consider typical, and the caged humans we call our neighbors, and perhaps count ourselves lucky to be among, seem content and well fed. But what if the wild beast that lurks within that doughnut maker were to be uncaged? A new humanity?

15 minutes, black and white. From the filmmaker, Ralph Arlyck.

Never Give Up

Never Give Up is the unlikely title for a sensitive and beautiful documentary about photographer Imogen Cunningham. If the popularity of a film depended on its artistic achievement alone, *Never Give Up* would become at least as popular as *Antonia*. In fact, both films are personal documentaries about an older woman highly skilled in her chosen art, yet underrated (if not unrecognized) by the general public. Both films take great care to reveal their subject as richly human, and both take the viewpoint of a former student paying homage.

The work of Imogen Cunningham spans half the life of the art itself. Born in 1883, she learned photography through a correspondence school course and self-teaching. She knows the rules of photography, as her photos clearly reveal, but it is her spirit that gives her art life. As she says, "I think I'm instinctive rather than go by rules." Her portrait work is admired throughout the world. She knows that photography is half psychology and that the problem in portraiture is that "nobody likes themself."

23 minutes, color, directed by Anne Hershey. From Phoenix Films; rental also from Viewfinders and University of California.

The New Boys

This film would make an excellent companion to the satire on the Kilgore Rangerettes, *Beauty Knows No Pain*. The new boys of this film are 13- and 14-year-old students of St. John's Cathedral School in Manitoba, Canada. They are made into "new boys" by an arduous 300-mile wilderness canoe trip (with stops only for food and sleep) designed to teach them responsibility and self-reliance.

Like the Kilgore Rangerettes, the new boys are subjected to demanding physical tasks that require them to demonstrate virtues appropriate to their sex. The Rangerettes are required always to smile and project "femininity"; the "new boys" are required to bear up under hardship and to "look after yourself because mommy won't remind you." Both schools see themselves as training grounds for adulthood, teaching survival skills for modern life.

St. John's Cathedral School was founded on the idea that "much of life has to be experienced to be understood." The wilderness canoe trip is presented as a kind of initiation, a deliverance into adulthood.

The New Boys is not a satirical film like *Beauty Knows No Pain*, and the two are more different than alike; yet they both shed different kinds of light on the subject of maturation. *The New Boys* also provokes thought and discussion about the concept of responsibility and self-reliance, the meaning of masculinity, the "school of hard knocks" and "sink or swim" as education, and what brings about maturation.

26 minutes, color, directed by John Smith, produced by National Film Board of Canada (1974). From Wombat Productions.

Next Door

Do you remember the first time that you were left alone at home while your parents went out for the night? You probably turned the radio or TV up loud to provide companionship and drown out all those strange noises and bumps in the night. That's exactly what the young boy does in *Next Door*, an adaptation of Kurt Vonnegut's short story.

The radio serves to bring into the story All Night Sam, a disc jockey who spins requests along with his own homey philosophy. Competing with All Night Sam is the couple in the next apartment. They argue about living together. She wants to move out of the apartment; he does not. The boy decides to quell the rising anger from the thin walls by phoning in a request to All Night Sam in the name of the neighbors—Mr. and Mrs. Harger. Sam thinks the boy is trying to bring his parents back together and gleefully plays the request, feeling he has done his good deed through the magic of radio. But the couple next door turns out to be Mr. Harger and a friend other than Mrs. Harger. They hear the request and find it less than funny; she runs out on Mr. Harger. Meanwhile, the real Mrs. Harger has heard the request on the radio and rushes back to tell hubby how much she loves him. So it goes, as Vonnegut would say.

Next Door is a good story and a typical Vonnegut commentary on loneliness and companionship. The boy has made the night for All Night Sam and Mrs. Harger. They no doubt lived happily ever after—at least for another night or two.

Andrew Silver directed *Next Door* as a videotape TV production for Boston Public TV station WGBH in 1975. The video-to-film transfer is of good quality. The acting is top-notch.

30 minutes, color. From Phoenix Films; rental also from Viewfinders.

Night and Fog

An international survey conducted by *Sight and Sound* magazine found *Night and Fog* ranked as one of the top 25 motion pictures ever made, feature films included.

The film documents the violence of the Nazi concentration camps as they existed in 1940. It begins in the present as the camera roams a now peaceful and deserted campsite to recreate the horrors of attempted genocide. The camera follows the death journey from the victims' arrival at the camp to the undressing for showers and the line to the gas chambers that look so much like innocent shower rooms. Grim reminders of the room's real purpose are found in the fingernail marks clawed into the stone ceiling. Actual documentary footage is shown of the condition of the dead, the living, and the living dead when the camps were liberated by the Allies. Pictures of piles of corpses and bits and pieces of once living human beings bulldozed into pits for graves are not for weak stomachs.

Yet the film's value in a classroom is not only in its ghastly horror footage but also in the later court scenes. Here the executioners say, "I am not responsible. I was only following orders." Each denies responsibility until there is no one left to bear it.

The final scene shifts to the camp twenty years later, now green and quiet. The narration leaves a warning; "Those of us who pretend to believe that all this happened only once, at a certain time and in a certain place, are those who refuse to see, who do not hear the cry to the end of time."

The question of responsibility and guilt is raised in *Night and Fog*, as it is in *Hangman* and *Interviews with My Lai Veterans*. If the concentration camps are viewed as a natural outcome of human nature and social forces instead of as a once-in-history aberration, the film becomes most valuable.

31 minutes, color and black and white, directed by Alain Resnais (1975). French with English subtitles. From Films Inc.; rental also from Viewfinders, University of California, University of Michigan.

Nixon: From Checkers to Watergate

If all the film footage ever made of Richard Nixon were laid head to tail, it would no doubt stretch from San Clemente to the White House and back again several times. Faced with such an overchoice, Charles Braverman could have made any film he wanted about the career of Richard Milhous Nixon. He could have made a compilation film called *A Comedy of Errors* or *An American Tragedy* or even *Something Wicked This Way Comes*. Instead, he has chosen a path of relative objectivity (perhaps no one can be entirely objective about

REPUBLICAN NATIO...

Richard Nixon until the twenty-first century), using film clips to illustrate both the heights of success and the depths of failure.

Braverman allows family pictures, films of early campaigns, and excerpts from speeches to talk for themselves. By its editing, the film draws attention to the consistency of the Nixon character from his Checker's speech to his disclaimers about Watergate. The film also juxtaposes speech excerpts to reveal Nixon as a public liar. But the overall tone of the film is surprisingly sympathetic to the man. Future generations watching *Nixon: From Checkers to Watergate* might have a hard time understanding why this decent, hardworking man was run out of the presidency for a few fibs in public. The film will disappoint those looking for a condensed version of *All the President's Men*, but it does serve as a handy summary of the career of one of America's most enigmatic presidents.

20 minutes, color, directed by Charles Braverman (1976). From Pyramid Films.

No Lies

No Lies is of interest for its film style as well as its subject matter—a woman's reaction to rape and her attempt to deny her own feelings.

The film is made in a fake *cinema verité* style so convincing and well-acted that few, if any, viewers will guess that it is scripted rather than spontaneous.

The cameraman/interviewer interacts with the woman, although he first intimidates her by asking "What's been happening in your life?" The woman moves from a response of "nothing much" to finally admitting "I was raped last week." The cameraman pressures her further, reduces her studied nonchalance to tears, and brings forth an admission of her anger and helplessness.

No Lies could be used in women's studies courses, but it is also an excellent study of the power of a camera to intimidate and of the ability of people to hide deep feelings behind masks of casualness.

16 minutes, color, directed by Mitchell Block (1973). From Phoenix Films; rental also from University of Michigan and Viewfinders.

No Reason to Stay

"The whole experience of secondary education . . . is set up in such a way as to insure that individual adolescents will become alienated from their own inner life; they are given no opportunity to examine it, and are punished if they permit it to direct their actions."

—*Edgar Z. Friendenberg*

A significant percentage of students who view *No Reason to Stay* will, if allowed, leap up and cheer wildly. They will proclaim that this is the first film that really tells it straight about school. The film was written by Christopher Wood, an intelligent high school dropout, to express his own feelings about school.

To Christopher, school is just another social structure to force him to conform. "No diploma, no job" is not a statement of common sense fact but a threat. His teachers expect Chris to be a bucket filling up with the knowledge that they want to pour in (like *the* four reasons for the fall of the Roman Empire). He resorts to creative daydreaming to escape the unreality of school but eventually decides to drop out.

His girl does not believe that he will drop out, his mother is convinced that as long as his grades are good nothing else could possibly be wrong, a counselor sputters helplessly when he announces his intentions, even the Canadian Cabinet tells him that dropouts aren't good for the nation.

He quits school because no one can offer him a reason to stay. His future is left undecided.

The film, which has the ability to bring to the surface similar feelings in other students, could be extremely valuable to the teacher who can understand such feelings. In many large cities, the average

IQ of dropouts is higher than that of those who stick it out, with the result that school is becoming an option rather than a taken-for-granted.

28 minutes, black and white (1966). From NFBC; rental also from University of California and University of Michigan.

Note from Above

Note from Above would make a most appropriate companion film for *The Lottery*. In this two-minute Derek Phillips animation, people's hands are seen through a stained glass window as they receive notes which come floating down from above. The first note reads, "I am the Lord"; the hands are shown praying. The second note commands, "Thou shalt have no other gods but me," and we see the hands throwing out statues and totem poles. Other notes float down, and the people respond by loving their neighbors and returning stolen property. The fifth note that comes down reads, "Thou shalt kill." The sixth floats quietly down and states, "Sorry, my mistake. That should have been: Thou shalt not kill." But there is no one left to receive the correction.

2 minutes, color, animated. From MMM.

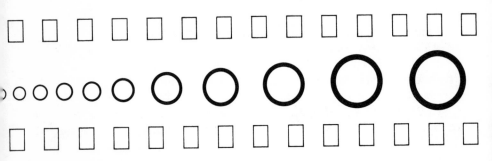

Obedience

This film is a plainly made documentary about the experiments of Dr. Stanley Milgram at Yale about thirteen years ago. He set out to discover how far people would be willing to go in the name of obedience.

Volunteers were told they were to take part in an experiment about the value of punishment in teaching. The volunteer was to help a "learner" (a person secretly in on the experiment) memorize a list of words by giving him shocks each time he recited the list incorrectly. With each mistake the shocks were to increase in intensity. The shock machine (a dummy that the subject was led to believe actually gave shocks) had a series of levers ranging from a tiny shock to one marked simply "XXX—Extreme Shock, Danger." The learner, who was concealed in a different room, communicated through a speaker. As the teacher gave more and more intense shocks, the learner was instructed to complain of a heart condition and plead to get out of the experiment.

The first two volunteers shown in the film stop short of "going all the way," but not without much hesitancy. The third volunteer, the film's main character, painfully makes his way up the row of switches. "I'm not gonna kill that man in there," he says. "I refuse to take the responsibility of his getting hurt in there." The attendant scientist tells him, "The experiment requires that you continue," and he does. At 420 volts, the man protests, "But he might be dead in there; I don't intend to be rude, but I think you should look in on him." He pulls all the levers, even the one marked XXX.

Before the experiment, psychologists were asked to predict how many subjects would go all the way on the machine. Their composite answer was that less than 1 percent would. The actual results? Fifty percent pulled all the levers in spite of the learner's pleas, groans, and final silence. The overall conclusion of the experiments is that "a substantial number of people do what they are told no matter what the content of the act."

Companion films such as *Interview with My Lai Veterans*, *Night and Fog*, or *Hangman* would make for a powerful unit on conformity and conscience.

45 minutes, black and white (1965). From New York University Film Library; rental also from University of Michigan.

Of Holes and Corks

This Zagreb Studio animation presents a battle between a man and some mysterious force shooting up from within the earth.

The man is relaxing in his walled yard, content that his high walls offer protection from the forces of evil. He is soon disturbed by a small geyser that pops up in the center of his enclosure. He promptly corks the geyser and returns to his newspaper. But another geyser springs up; again he corks it. For the next eight minutes geysers spring up all over the yard keeping the man constantly busy with corks.

His heavily protected yard is now a total shambles. Its walls are unable to cope with a force from within the earth that clearly needs to release pressure. Since his corks prevent the release his job is never-ending. He has made at least two mistakes; first, in walling himself in against a force that would "attack" from within and, second, in trying to prevent the escape of what must be released. His mistakes finally lead to destruction.

Each individual has a personal high wall of defenses that he believes offers protection. But no wall can protect against the pressure from within. Corks are an illusory solution, as are walls. The self-deception practiced by the man in the cartoon is one that is common to every person.

10 minutes, color, animation. From International Film Bureau; rental also from University of California.

Omega

This is a visually magnificent short film—the *2001* of the short film. It could become a classic among film study groups and an inspiration for amateur filmmakers who have limited funds and equipment. Made by UCLA student Donald Fox, it consists almost totally of special effects—many of them achieved with little more than kitchen equipment. The end result is as professional as that of films made with enormous budgets.

Omega deals with the end of man in an evolutionary sense: his rebirth and liberation from planet earth. By sending an "energy ray" to the sun and harnessing its solar power, man is transformed in a single leap. The film, which contains visual, audio, and thematic references to Kubrick's *2001*, is more a "trip," or visual experience, than a documentary or a story.

Like Kubrick's work, *Omega* will probably evoke a more enthusiastic response from young people than from adults. If you show it, be sure to do so on as large a screen as possible and make the room as dark as you can. A small image in a partially lit room will reduce the film's total impact.

13 minutes, color. From Pyramid Films; rental also from the University of California, University of Michigan, and Viewfinders.

One Day More

On the surface, *One Day More* is simply a film essay about the mud baths near Bujanovic, Yugoslavia. The baths are purported to be able to heal incurable diseases. But on a deeper level, *One Day More* is a profound film about creation, human community, ritual, and faith.

The film begins in darkness and silence. A line of mud-covered bodies crawls through the ooze and vapor. The brilliantly filmed scene is reminiscent of Dante's *Inferno*, but here, instead of fire there is mud, instead of damnation there is re-creation. Gradually, Ligeti-type choral music is added to the track, and the bodies come to life as individuals, rubbing mud on afflicted parts, feeling themselves, even smoking a cigarette. There is an air of expectancy but no communication. Once the people ascend from the mud and begin to cleanse themselves, a sense of community develops, and we see that these are ordinary people, not strange or grotesque creatures. The final shot is of a young girl combing the knots from her hair. We realize that the mud has somehow changed the bathers; it does indeed heal. These are not superstitious European peasants but contemporary human beings who know the meaning of water and earth and its ability to re-create. They are aware of the healing power of ritual, of descent and ascent, of baptism, of primal ooze, and of a community joined by faith and basic humanity.

One Day More is a masterpiece of artistic economy and a film that truly uses the power of cinema to its best advantage. Discussion possibilities are endless, and the film could easily serve as an example to would-be filmmakers of how to speak eloquently the language of cinema.

10 minutes, color, directed by Vlatko Gilic (1972). From McGraw-Hill Films.

Order in the House

Society as seen through the eyes of a law-and-order garbage collector is the subject of this Hungarian animated gem. The antihero garbage collector believes that people are like animals and that a strong hand is all they need to keep them in line. He would like to impose a system based on garbage usage. The "most garbage people" should live on the first floor, those who are sloppy with garbage should be noted in a book, and those who are really rotten should be sent to special houses.

The garbage man's system is frightening, his respect for individual liberty nonexistent. Because he's only a garbage man, his views might easily be dismissed. But who is to say that judging people by their garbage is any less rational than pigeon-holing them by I.Q., financial status, color, or religion? And isn't every man's view of the world affected by his position in it, by his contact with a limited reality? Whether doctor or garbage man, he tends to see things as "he is," not as "they are."

The superb animation technique of *Order in the House* communicates as much as does the monologue of the garbage man. The distributor claims that the visual technique suggests Ernst Trova's *Falling Man*, but I find it reminiscent of early animation by Peter Foldes.

5 minutes, color, animated. From LCA.

Organism

It has become commonplace to view cities with disdain as chaotic places of unplanned growth. But is it possible that we have actually fashioned cities as unwitting monuments to our own bodies? Have we taken what we know of our bodily functions, translated them into concrete and steel, and called the resulting creation a city? Screening Hilary Harris's film, *Organism*, suggests that we have indeed created cities in our own image and likeness.

Time-lapse photography of the flow of people and traffic in cities is juxtaposed with microphotography of the human bloodstream, nervous system, and skeletal structure to draw the metaphor. Both bodies and cities have systems to provide for fuel, elimination, reproduction, maintenance, and repair. Streets are arteries, people and cars are blood and corpuscles, construction is reproduction, buildings are skeletal structures, police and fire officers fight crime and disaster much as white corpuscles fight disease, and a traffic jam is comparable to cancer.

The film's sparse narration (which, unfortunately, is difficult to hear) suggests less obvious extensions of the city/body metaphor. As the camera shows the seemingly mindless but highly patterned flow of people on streets, for example, it observes about the central nervous system that its "vast amount of activity is automatic."

Organism is simple and yet profound, with a theme that only film can capture with such beauty and impact.

20 minutes, color, directed by Hilary Harris (1975). From Phoenix Films; rental also from Viewfinders.

The Owl

The Owl is a chilling, startling reminder that the romantic, benevolent view of nature so popular now is part truth and part self-deception. This Yugoslavian film presents a more tooth-and-claw view of nature, where only the fittest and the luckiest survive.

An owl attacks a nest of newborn blackbirds and slowly eats them with all the regret of a gourmet attacking a châteaubriand. The blood-red eyes of this professional assassin fill the screen and blink calmly as if to verify that his act of murder is simply part of the cycle of life in nature. Slowly, hordes of blackbirds gather to defend the nest. They swoop down on the owl like planes strafing a target and finally beat the gorged owl to the ground where he flaps off wounded. The battle ends with the usual toll of dead and wounded.

The cinematography in *The Owl* is incredible, especially to a generation raised on Disney nature films and Sunday-afternoon outdoorsman shows on TV. *The Owl* would make a nice companion film to *BLT*. Discussion possibilities include one's personal concept of nature and the image of nature usually presented in films.

11 minutes, color, directed by Aleksander Illic at Dunav Films. From International Film Bureau.

Pain: Where Does It Hurt Most?

This film is an NBC-TV documentary exploring pain. Pain is a universal experience and yet remains a mystery even to modern science. Since Americans receive $2.5 billion in compensation for work lost because of pain, it is obviously a national health problem. In spite of its universality and crippling potential, doctors know so little about it that their almost invariable recourse is to prescribe a pill (over a billion are used every year).

Pain explores exceptions to the pill remedy at three institutions in the vanguard of pain research. At Seattle's Pain Clinic, the main principle of treatment is that pain must not be rewarded and patients are never asked how they feel. A woman in constant pain is shown moaning in her bed. Doctors standing around her tell her that she is doing fine and improving in her use of the "moan machine." The moan machine is a device that measures the frequency of a patient's moans. When the number of moans-per-hour falls below a certain level, the patient is rewarded by a light. To viewers the treatment seems crude and even cruel. But after many other attempts had failed, two weeks at the pain clinic cured this particular patient. The clinic functions on the assumption that pain, when no organic cause can be found, is a learned response and therefore can be unlearned.

The film shows other patients unlearning pain and explores the "gate control" theory of pain and the relationship of pain to pleasure. The "gate control" theory states that a big pain can be stopped by inducing a lot of small pains. The theory might explain a person's biting his lips when under stress, rubbing a bruise, or even finding relief through acupuncture.

Pain: Where Does It Hurt Most? is a fascinating documentary about an important and often overlooked topic.

51 minutes, color, directed by Tom Priestly (1972). From Films Inc.; rental also from University of Michigan.

The Parting

Death in America is no longer a call from the divine or a mysterious event. It has become a problem in engineering—how to dispose of the dead with as little discomfort to the living as possible. But in more primitive parts of the world, death is an accepted part of life and is ritually commemorated. *The Parting* masterfully presents the funeral ritual of the common people in the Montenegro region of Yugoslavia. The contrast to the American way of death is so striking as to challenge beliefs about the proper commemoration of death in the family.

Inside a room lit by a fireplace, people gather around a dead man. The body is undressed and the old clothing burned and replaced by a colorful outfit that far surpasses in luxury the dress of any of the living. There is much waiting around. The men smoke and drink silently; a photographer snaps a carefully posed family picture; coffee grounds left in cups are read; the women kiss the forehead of the dead man and leave an offering. Slowly the mood changes from funeral quiet to lively companionship—the wake becomes a communion.

At the cemetery both men and women wail in a stylized manner, expressing their sorrow as a formal community. The film ends as it began, showing the ordinary way of life in the village.

This 1973 Zagreb film is carefully constructed to make the viewer a participant in the ceremony. *The Parting* uses only natural sounds and visuals to tell its story. No narrated film could match the depth of its comment about the acceptance of death. It deserves a number of viewings and much discussion; opportunities to compare the Montenegrins' death ritual with our own usual practices abound. *The Parting*, in short, is one of the finest films available for a unit in death education.

16 minutes, color (1973). From Wombat Productions.

Peege

Peege is a film that deserves to become an educational classic. After a viewing, half the class will be near tears, but they will spread the word and students will come from nowhere to ask to see the film they've heard so much about. High school students seasoned on many films selected it as one of the three best of the 1972–73 school year.

Peege is the story of a family's Christmas visit to an old age home for a last meeting with their dying Grandma. The parents and two teenage boys approach the home with such thoughts as "Can she see anymore?" and "How long will she last?" They enter the home as the sounds of *The Dating Game* on TV drift cruelly through the lobby.

Peege doesn't recognize her family; she sits strapped to her chair, kept alive by tubes in her veins, by memories, and by pure habit. The parents try—with the desperation the young feel when faced with the old—to talk to Peege. They give simple gifts and "report" on their activities. Peege nods occasionally, but there is no real contact. Finally the mother cries (does she sees something of herself strapped in that chair?), and the father announces an acceptable excuse for their departure. They kiss Peege ever so dutifully, as if they feared her age to be a contagious disease. Such family dramas are enacted millions of times yearly in rest homes.

But Greg, the oldest son, stays behind. Since the morning, Greg has been reliving boyhood memories of Grandma. Through flashbacks we learn that Peege was quite a robust, loving, and earthy Grandma who gave much to her grandson. Greg bends close to Peege and tells her, "I know somewhere inside there is the Grandma I remember." He speaks of his memories and shares his feelings and tells Peege he loves her. Finally Peege smiles.

Peege is a film about honest communication across the chasm between youth and age. The inability to communicate with the very old is an unrecognized national crisis. One of every ten Americans is over 65. In the minds of many, these 20 million people comprise a class of feared and rejected aliens. The young cannot confront the old without being reminded of their own future membership in this class and of its closeness to death. *Peege* will not solve the communication crisis, but it is one of the few films to recognize its existence and to suggest a solution in deeply touching terms.

All the characters in this highly professional film are played by well-known figures from TV and the movies, who handle their roles with unusual skill.

28 minutes, color, written and directed by Randal Kleiser (1973). From Phoenix Films; rental also from University of California and Viewfinders.

Pegasus

The Belgian animator, Raoul Servais, is best known for his *Chromophobia, Sirene,* and *Goldframe.* In *Pegasus,* he has created a parable about technology and the human spirit. A blacksmith with little left to do watches mechanical reapers efficiently harvest wheat. His attention is distracted only by a pesky fly that he attempts to kill with a heavy hammer.

To fill the vacuum created by technology, the blacksmith decides to build a shrine to the vanished past. He constructs a huge horse's head and worships it religiously. When rain comes, his shrine grows and magically reproduces. When it begins to overrun the wheat fields, the blacksmith becomes frightened. Like the sorcerer's apprentice or Doctor Frankenstein, he has created a monster that has a life of its own. His reaction to this miracle of creation is to hide in his shop and return to the distraction-become-obsession of killing flies with a hammer.

Pegasus is certainly not destined to rival the writing of Mary Shelley or the stories of the Greek mythologists, but it is an outstanding example of the animation parable with darkly ambiguous overtones.

The blacksmith is clearly unable to adapt to the mechanized horses that have taken over the fields. His efforts to kill a fly with a hammer symbolize his unwillingness to consider alternatives or to change the tools that have made his life. Instead, he turns the past into a religion that becomes as much of a threat as the mechanical horses. His plight is not so different from that of many nations or individuals who condemn themselves to the past and create their own monsters in the face of technological change.

Servais's masterly animation technique effectively captures mythic echoes of the winged Pegasus and Orestes.

9 minutes, color. From International Film Bureau.

The Persistent Seed

Hundreds of films tell of the human destruction of nature and warn against human folly. Only a handful use the poetry of film to compose a paean to the tenacity of life. *The Persistent Seed* is such a meditation.

This National Film Board of Canada presentation is about the creation of tomorrow as it quietly takes place today, about the tough but tiny seed of life that survives in spite of monstrous obstacles. It is a film about survival, about huge drop forges and delicate flowers, about children playing in lawn sprinklers and being re-created along with the grass, about people in concrete canyons planting flowers on window sills to remind them of life.

The color and sepia cinematography overflows with the loving eye of the artist. No narration or dramatic musical score is needed to carry the film's power. *The Persistent Seed* is a hymn of praise that touches that spot in each viewer where there still remains a childlike love of nature.

14 minutes, color, directed by Christopher Chapman (1963). From NFBC.

The Plutocrats

The Plutocrats is a BBC documentary that takes a fascinating and oh-so-British look at the foibles and excesses of four Texas multimillionaires. Amazingly, all four allowed the BBC crew to film them at work and at home.

The first of these plutocrats, Harold Byrd, demonstrates his acute sense of values by observing that "a handkerchief that sells for $500 is an expensive handkerchief." Having thus established himself as just another average millionaire, he flies from oil well to oil well in his fifty-eighth airplane. When not inspecting his wealth, he hunts. At one point he proudly proclaims, "I don't think I've ever shot anything edible." His wife enters the sumptuous trophy room to explain how she ordered a wig for a stuffed lion.

Mrs. Byrd could have ordered the wig from the store of the second plutocrat—Stanley Marcus of Nieman-Marcus fame. Marcus takes viewers on a tour of his store to show them the "incomparables"— items for sale that are the best of their kind in existence. He admits that since many Nieman-Marcus customers have everything, the store tries to find things that they don't have—an elephant, say.

The late H.L. Hunt lived in a house modeled after Mount Vernon, took his lunch to work in a brown paper bag, and allowed himself few pleasures in spite of his $225,000 a day income. He appears in this film as a gentle, doddering old man but was thought by many during his life to be the most dangerous of the millionaires because of the people he backed with his wealth. He divided mankind into two groups—Communists and anti-Communists—and railed against the U.N., Medicare, and all forms of government aid. His "Lifeline" radio program has been aired on as many as 400 stations.

Roy Mark Hofheinz is the builder of the Astrodome and perhaps the world's greatest living showman. He has already bought the Barnum and Bailey Circus and is now at work building an Astroworld that will make Disneyland look like just another traveling carnival.

Some viewers see such millionaires as living testimonies to the ability of wealth to corrupt. Others see them as the epitome of the wildest of their American Dreams.

51 minutes, color. From Time-Life Films.

Post No Bills

Post No Bills is about a fellow who goes around burning down billboards in the name of keeping America beautiful and free from commercialism. Just watching him destroy a billboard is loads of fun. But he finally gets caught and is led peacefully to a small town for booking and perhaps a jail sentence.

As he emerges from the City Hall, he is greeted as a hero and taken to the local bar for a celebration. The next scene shows our rebel hero on a television talk show. As he joins the other guests and sits down, he lights a cigarette. Freeze frame, lose color, zoom back to reveal this

same pose with lighted cigarette six feet high on a billboard. Print on the billboard reads: "Smoke the Rebel's Cigarette."

Post No Bills is a film about commitment and co-option. To be radically committed to any movement for basic change in America today is like trying to punch one's way out of a marshmallow. Every blow against the status quo returns not change but sweet success; every hack at the root draws not blood but fame and fortune. Yesterday's underground becomes today's best seller and tomorrow's cliché. From rock music to Jerry Rubin to peace symbol bath mats, co-option is a threat to commitment.

Post No Bills is an excellent film, fast paced and entertaining, complete with a surprise ending.

10 minutes, color. From MMM.

The Prejudice Film

Every now and then an "instructional" film comes along that is both educational and entertaining. *The Prejudice Film* is one of them and deals with a vital topic as well. It begins with a series of ethnic jokes that are followed by vignettes illustrating racial prejudice in school situations. To raise the level of consideration above only racial prejudice, viewers see a confused Aristotle in an American restaurant and some equally bewildered Americans confronted by French cuisine.

Narrator David Hartman asks the film's basic question, "Where does prejudice come from?" In answer, he explains that even babies tend to reject strangers and that we all feel a little uptight around that which is strange. He further suggests that overly strict parents produce kids with a suppressed anger that is later directed at underdogs and that children unconsciously accept the prejudices that their parents pass along.

The film examines the various levels of prejudice—vocal prejudice, avoidance, active participation, violence, and finally killing. *The Prejudice Film* points out that the most dehumanizing aspect of prejudice is that its practioners must first devalue those they hate and make them less than human. The film concludes by showing great works of art by "niggers, spics, and polacks."

Fast pacing, excellent insights into the psychology of prejudice, believable situations, and a sense of humor make this a fine film.

28 minutes, color. From Motivational Media.

Productivity and the Self-Fulfilling Prophecy: The Pygmalion Effect

This CRM (*Psychology Today*) film was made as an aid for management-training courses. Happily, it is general enough in approach to be very valuable for teacher training or even high school and college psychology classes.

The film explains the concept of the self-fulfilling prophecy or the "Pygmalion Effect"—the notion that the prediction or expectation of an event can actually cause it to happen. The film combines a variety of techniques—interviews with authorities, animation, historical film clips, even a brief section of *My Fair Lady*—to present both the theory and practical application of this phenomenon. The film even explains how to become a "positive pygmalion" in order to improve one's own performance or behavior or that of fellow students or employees.

The Pygmalion Effect seems to thrive in schools. In the mid-1960s, Robert Rosenthal and Lenore Jacobson tested the Pygmalion Effect in an elementary school in a lower-class neighborhood. At the beginning of the school year they gave all the children a nonverbal IQ test. They announced that the test results could predict "intellectual blooming." After the test, they randomly chose 20 percent of the children in each class and labeled them intellectual "bloomers." Rosenthal and Jacobson told the teachers that these children could be expected to show remarkable gains during the coming year on the basis of their test scores. In actuality, the difference between these experimental children and the control group existed solely in the teachers' minds.

Push

Push is similar enough to the old *Have I Told You Lately That I Love You?* to be considered almost a remake of that student classic. In *Push*, a central character goes through a day while the camera focuses on his relation to machines. Later, the film attempts to show how the concept of "pushing buttons" is somehow related to pushiness in personal relations and to pollution. It is in this second part that *Push* bites off more than it can digest. *Have I Told You Lately* concentrated on one clear idea and presented that effectively. *Push* tries too hard to say something significant about technology, personal relations, *and* pollution—all in nine minutes.

A comparison of the two films would make a valuable unit in a film study class since they are very similar in theme yet very different in approach.

9 minutes, color, directed and photographed by Urs Furrer, the cinematographic director of the feature film Shaft (1972). *From Wombat Productions; rental also from University of California.*

Quasi at the Quackadero

Quasi is a kid of the future who lives with robot Rollo and an adult of unspecified relationship with the plebeian name of Anita. For a day's outing, they fly to the Quackadero, a Coney Island of the future. Here they can watch people relive moments from their past in "Your Shining Moment" or enter the Hall of Time Mirrors and see themselves at every age. The "Think Blink" produces pictures of their thoughts; another "ride" gives them a chance to see last night's dreams today and also gives animator Sally Cruikshank her best chance to show off her creative animation.

The fun and games at the Quackadero represent not so much the technical advances of the future as they do an extension of today's carnival quackery. The Quackadero is an elaborate carnival sideshow rather than a real futureworld.

The children were retested eight months later. The experime
children (intellectual bloomers) showed an overall IQ gain of
points more than the control children—two points in verbal al
and seven points in reasoning. Test results were the same whe
the child was in a high-ability or low-ability classroom.

Perhaps the most remarkable finding was that the teachers
sonal attitudes had also been affected. They thought the bri
students were more appealing, more affectionate, and l
adjusted than the other students. Of course, there were som
dents who had gained in IQ even though they had not been
nated as intellectual bloomers. Ironically, the teachers found
students not as well adjusted, interesting, or affectionate as
the students who had not done well. Thus, it was not the increa
that caused the teachers to like or dislike their pupils but whe
not they had done what had been predicted of them.

Productivity and the Self-Fulfilling Prophecy is an imj
film in psychology with a wide variety of applications. It is wel
and expertly written.

30 minutes, color, directed by Joan Owens (1974)
McGraw-Hill Films; rental also from University of Californi

Prometheus XX

Prometheus XX is a Bulgarian animation that changes Pro
from the tragic hero of traditional myth into a tragicomic an
Chaplinesque Prometheus with a broad smile and red hai
from the Olympians, whose fire he has stolen. As he runs t
his torch to humanity, he passes a timeless landscape th
places the film in both antiquity and the twentieth (XX)
When he nears a city, a fireman's hose douses the flame. Ur
he again steals fire and returns; this time he is mugged. Af
theft, he presents his torch to an emperor, who turns out t
the world's most notorious pyromaniac. As the film
twentieth-century Prometheus is trying again.

The torch's flame radiates various symbols: vitality, pe
and spirituality—the Promethean spirit. The three failure
human flaws that have prevented the potential of the
developing. The film poses the question: Will our Promett
tial or our shadow side prevail?

Prometheus XX is rich in mythical allusions, symbc
meaning, and comic devices. Todor Dinov's art work is
and his direction faultless.

6 minutes, animated, color. From Wombat Produc

Quasi is similar in "plot" to the Firesign Theater recording, *I Think We're All Bozos on This Bus.* The ideas and animation are fascinating, but the humor exists in a netherworld between sublety and broad satire. A Firesign Theater on film it is not.

10 minutes, color, animation, directed by Sally Cruikshank. From Pyramid Films; rental also from University of California.

The Question of Television Violence

The Question of Television Violence is a report on the 1972 U.S. Senate hearings on television violence conducted by Senator Pastore.

The well-edited version of the four-day hearings features the U.S. Surgeon General, who states positively that, contrary to general opinion, "televised violence does indeed have an adverse effect on those children predisposed to violence." He points out that many people read "predisposed to violence" as "abnormal" whereas in reality "we don't know who is predisposed or how many are so."

Nicholas Johnson also appears before the committee and states that "if you do child molesting on a weekday on a playground, you get driven off to jail. If you molest millions on a Saturday morning, you get driven off in a long black limousine." Sitting near Johnson is his boss, FCC chairman Dean Burch, who explains, "We're not impressed by the conclusions of Mr. Johnson." Senate committee member Howard Baker, of Watergate fame, takes issue with Johnson's child molesting analogy, and the two engage in a lively verbal jousting match.

Peggy Charren from *Action for Children's Television* appears to present her sane proposals for the reform of children's programming.

Finally, the presidents of the three networks and the NAB appear before the fatherly Sen. Pastore (who sounds and looks a bit like a young Groucho Marx), who takes them to task for a do-nothing attitude. The presidents of CBS and NBC act a bit like children on the losing end of a scolding from their parents. But Elton Rule, president of ABC, promises concrete reforms backed by a million-dollar research study.

The film moves quickly considering that the only action is people talking. The American public proved by watching the Watergate hearings in droves that even a stuffy Senate hearing can be as entertaining as the best soap opera. *The Question of Television Violence* just might be the most revealing film in existence about television.

55 minutes, color, produced by The National Film Board of Canada. From Phoenix Films, rental also from Viewfinders.

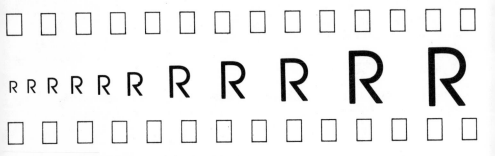

The Reason Why

The Reason Why is a one-act play written for the screen by Arthur Miller. Miller says about the film, "What I wanted to put down are the facts, the way we're made, the impulses of the human animal toward war. . . ." The story involves two men, one the owner of a farm, the other a friend visiting from the city. As they sit outside talking, a woodchuck "damn near big as a raccoon" appears about 350 yards away. The owner tells how one year he killed 42 chucks in order to protect his vegetable garden. The two compare killing animals to human warfare, and the owner recounts how his "limited war" on the woodchucks developed into a real hatred until finally he realized that with "what it cost to kill them I could have bought enough tomatoes for the year."

Both men show little interest in hunting, but they finally agree to take a shot at the woodchuck. The owner brings out his $65 rifle with telescopic sight and drills the chuck in the head. "Why'd you do that," the visitor asks. "I don't know, I probably won't anymore," he replies. But viewers know that he will shoot more woodchucks.

The many obvious parallels to human warfare in the story provide excellent discussion material. The film rates only a B− in production values, but the story comes through unscathed. Very usable in conjunction with the short story classic, "The Most Dangerous Game," and Robert Sheckley's short story, "The Seventh Victim," in his *Untouched by Human Hands* (Ballantine paperback). Both stories involve man as the hunter and the hunted.

13 minutes, color, directed by Paul Leaf. From BFA.

The Resurrection of Broncho Billy

Produced as a workshop project by seniors at USC, this film won a 1970 Academy Award as the best live-action short subject and picked up a handful of less prestigious awards as well.

Resurrection is about Billy, a would-be cowboy who rides the wide open prairies of Los Angeles, fights imaginary gun duels with businessmen passing on the sidewalk, and lives a fantasy life of himself as Jimmy Stewart, John Wayne, and Gary Cooper all rolled into one. In reality Billy (played by Johnny Crawford of *Rifleman* fame) is just a kid who never grew out of the boyhood phase of hero worship and imitation. He is unable to face the fact that he is as far from being a tough cowboy as Roy Rogers was from being a suave desperado.

Billy gets up in the morning and begins a day of continuous failure. First he is harassed by his landlady; then he loses his job. He enters a bar, plops down a coin, and says, "Gimme a redeye;" but the bartender replies, "You're gonna need some ID, kid." Outside the bar, Billy finally meets a pair of real-life, pot-bellied bad guys who beat and rob him. He shakes off this attack on his fantasy and orders a soft drink, telling the girl at the stand, "I've just been in one hell of a fight," but her only response is, "That'll be twenty cents." He sheepishly remembers that he has no money.

The girl asks to sketch him in his Western duds and he consents. But he is dissatisfied when she sketches him as he is, not as a personification of the Old West. She tires of his monologue and walks off. But even this rejection doesn't phase Billy. The film turns from its sepia tint to full color as he imagines himself on a horse, swooping up the girl and riding off into the sunset.

The themes of the film are the life of fantasy, the imitation of movie heroes, and the passing of the Old West. Producer John Longenecker (whose father conveniently operates a Hollywood talent agency) and director James Rokos spent only $700 making the 21-minute short. The film — technically better than most student efforts, although its sparse dialogue is difficult to understand — is shot in a classic Western style with sharp angle shots, tight close-ups, and even a suspenseful dolly shot.

Did *Resurrection* deserve an Academy Award? It certainly is a nicely crafted student exercise and shows talent, but it is far from the best live-action short of 1970.

21 minutes, sepia and color (1970). From USC.

The Return

Scary movies have been rediscovered in the late 1970s, and *The Return* has to stand as one of the best and scariest. Stephen Royds, nicely played by Peter Vaughan, calls at night at a desolate, boarded-up Edwardian mansion. Mrs. Park, the caretaker, shows him around after he expresses an interest in buying the house.

Royds prods Mrs. Park into telling the story of the house, and viewers learn that its last owner, a man named Harboys, had murdered his wife there and had been put into an asylum for the rest of his life. Royds reveals that rumors of the appearance of the wife's ghost

have brought him to the house to prove Harboys's innocence. Royds is, of course, Harboys himself, returned to the scene of the crime to confront the ghost. He bribes Mrs. Park to let him spend the night in the wedding chamber where the murder took place. Armed with a gun, he shuts himself in the room and waits.

The ending is a nicely understated shock that is as terrifying for what it does not reveal as much as for what it does.

The Return features excellent cinematography, in which every angle, shot, and shadow contribute to the mood of impending doom. The film is a combination of two short stories—A.M. Burrage's "Nobody's House" and Ambrose Bierce's "The Middle Toe of the Right Foot." The film would make an excellent study of literature-to-film adaptation, as well as a case study in mood and lighting.

30 minutes color, directed by Sture Rydman (1976). From Pyramid Films.

Return of the Kitemen

What books are to Ray Bradbury in the dystopia of *Fahrenheit 451*, kites are to director David McNicoll in this film about an Orwellian futureworld. A man named Henry lives in a "maximum deviation area" where residents have a comparatively high degree of freedom. But the totalitarian state controls its citizens through police and detailed instructions delivered on television. Children are sent to "guidance," people are required to use "respirators," pacification is offered in the form of authorized drugs and channel "goodfeel" on TV, which offers a "sex function mode." Language has been reduced to a barebones newspeak, in which adjectives and adverbs are nearly useless.

Henry awakes from a dream of the freedom of the old days. He finds that someone has sent him a kite, but his wife warns him: "Dreams deviant, kite deviant." He goes out to try to fly the kite in spite of his wife's warning of "imperative destruct." When his efforts fail, he visits Amberg, an aging eccentric, who is retired from his government post as minister of aerial pastimes. Amberg tells Henry, "Never run with a kite; you can't force a kite to fly. Let it find its own current." So Henry tries again.

This time his wife and children watch, horrified at Henry's dangerously deviant behavior, yet responsive to the beauty of the kite and the balance it strikes between freedom and control, a balance that is totally lacking in their repressive society. Kites have been banned because they contain a message; they demonstrate the exhilaration that comes from working in concert with nature. Such a message is taboo in a society that cannot afford to recognize individuals.

But as the message of the kite dawns on Henry and his family, the police arrive to take him away for a "tertiary guidance tour." The police explain in their own doublespeak, "A kite is self-oriented and so is wrong. We remember what happened. Not enough to go around. Now we've stopped that. There is enough if there are no more me's. It is a symptom of the old ways—me alone. We must protect new people from knowledge of old ways."

As they lead Henry away, another kite is seen floating on the horizon. There is still hope.

Return of the Kitemen is an ambitious film. Others such as Orwell, Bradbury, and Huxley have dealt with the same themes with far greater depth and understanding. But for a short film, *Return of the Kitemen* offers solid entertainment, compelling visuals and sounds, mental provocation, and plenty of material for discussion. The film is very useful for future studies, a study of the individual versus the demands of the state, totalitarianism, the possible effects of "lifeboat ethics," and for comparison with other dire warnings about the future.

30 minutes, color, directed by David McNicoll (1974). From Phoenix Films; rental also from Viewfinders.

Rhinoceros

"The rhinoceros is the man with preconceived ideas."
        —*Eugene Ionesco, author of the play,* Rhinoceros

In the opening scene of this simply animated film, a group of people is shown making the usual meaningless small talk about everything and nothing. Those who don't talk dream lazily or read newspapers detailing the daily butchery and death. No one seems too disturbed when a rhinoceros rumbles past.

The scene changes to an office and the ever-present griping about work and boredom. The boss enters in the form of a rhinoceros. Later, at a play, the entire audience, with the exception of a single man, grows a rhinoceros horn for a nose. The lone nonconformist worries about his abnormality—everyone else has a horn, why not he? Eventually, the rhinoceroses take over the world.

Ionesco claims that he chose the rhinoceros for his image because he wanted a narrow-minded animal that charges straight ahead. He later admits that the more exact choice would have been a sheep; "My rhinoceroses are sheep that become mad." The rhinoceros mentality is what the film is about. Even virtue can become a rhinoceros. The most immediate theme of the film that students will grasp is the danger of conformity. Some study of Ionesco's work would be helpful in understanding the film at a deeper level.

11 minutes, color, animation, directed by Jan Lenica (1964). From McGraw-Hill Films; rental also from University of California.

The Rocking-Horse Winner

Learning Corporation of America has produced a series of short films based on well-known short stories. The series, "Classics: Dark and Dangerous," includes this interpretation of D.H. Lawrence's "The Rocking-Horse Winner."

In the world of feature films, it is almost a truism that truly classic films will never be made by interpreting novels, and this truism applies equally to short films. The best short films are original filmic ideas, rather than interpretations of literature. Most stories lose something in their translation to the screen. When dealing with a D.H. Lawrence story, such a loss is inevitable. Why a teacher of either film or literature would want to show a 30-minute film of a 15-page story I don't know—perhaps to motivate nonreaders.

The film version of *The Rocking-Horse Winner* is not a bad film (although its maker could be faulted for overuse of the wide-angle lens and for trying to make all the interior shots look like scenes from *Citizen Kane*); it just does not bring to life the special world of D.H. Lawrence. It faithfully conveys the plot of his story but little more. The film must ultimately be seen as a marketable product for the school audience rather than as a work motivated by true creative enthusiasm (to borrow an idea from Abel Gance), or by the dictates of art.

Even with these criticisms, it stands as a good story, useful for discussion or perhaps as a way to introduce D.H. Lawrence to a young audience.

The story tells of a boy, Paul, who lives in a house divided by the need for more money. To his parents, luck is "what causes you to have money. If you're lucky, you have money. That's why it's better to be born lucky than rich. If you're rich, you may lose your money. But if you're lucky, you will always get more money." Paul decides that he will be lucky and rides his rocking-horse feverishly in order to arrive at that place called "luck." His secret, frenzied excursions on his horse enable him to predict racehorse winners. He gives some of his winnings from bets to his mother, disguising them as an anonymous donation, but he finds that the money seems only to make her more unhappy.

One night, Paul's mother discovers him on one of his feverish rides and watches as he rocks himself into unconsciousness. As he falls from the rocking-horse, he screams, "It's Malabar." Paul's father shrewdly places money on Malabar. When news of Malabar's win is brought to Paul's bedside, he is free to die.

The Rocking-Horse Winner is open to a variety of interpretations, most of which require some familiarity with the work of D.H. Lawrence and access to the original short story. The study guide with the film suggests that such interpretations are available to viewers—a suggestion best left to more advanced students who would be better off reading the original story. The translation of short stories into short films is an intriguing project. Even with their artistic results predictably mixed, such films as The Rocking-Horse Winner can be useful to teachers and educators on at least an introductory level.

29 minutes, color, directed by Peter Medak. From LCA.

Rumors of War

Rumors of War is reminiscent of War Games in its theme and typically British understatement but lacks the gut excitement of the latter. Rumors of War is the story of the nuclear arms race. Presenting a cross section of public reaction to the continued development of atomic weapons, the one-hour documentary manages to be both engrossing and frightening.

Combining footage shot at missile installations with models and animation, the film surveys the development of the atomic weapon from World War II to its present capability and future potential. Noting that there now exists the nuclear equivalent of ten tons of T.N.T. for every person on earth, opponents contend that progress in the arms race means less, not greater, security for everyone. Defense officials insist that extensive precautions have been instituted to prevent "doomsday" from occurring. They demonstrate "fail-safe" measures at a Minute-Man missile installation and display the computer network which detects attack.

Critics of the weapons race point out that nuclear submarines have no such fail-safe systems and that a missile launch is solely at a captain's discretion. They also fear that computer errors could lead to an atomic holocaust. One official offers a solution to such fears with the words: "You either use computers or a preprogrammed President."

60 minutes, color, a BBC-TV production. From Time-Life Films.

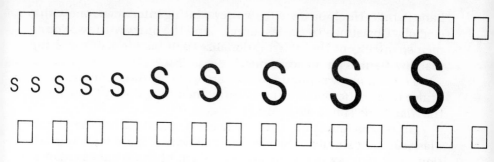

Saturday Afternoon

In *Saturday Afternoon*, mime is used as a vehicle for a parable about familial role-playing and the escape from life via television. The film's impact doesn't come from the plot but from the mechanical movements of the mime couple.

A man sprawls in his chair, drinking beer, switching channels on the TV while showing boredom, envy, delight, desire, and frustration as he watches the commercials flit across the screen. His wife also watches, in between dusting and running the sweeper, looking longingly at the TV ad for the perfect Hawaiian vacation.

Their son, the only "real" person, is outside trying to blow a trumpet. He comes in to show off for his parents, but his attention is captured instead by the football game on TV. The father then takes the son out to the garage to demonstrate his strength but fails to match the feats of the two-inch figures running across the screen. But the son still accepts his dad, and his loyalty acts as a catalyst that brings the parents "back to life." The dad returns to the living room and dances with his wife in a scene that resembles two mannequins who have received a soul transplant.

The film is intended to lead to discussions about living life versus watching it, about the lack of communication in a family whose members play restricted roles, and about acceptance of individuals for what they are.

11 minutes, color, directed by John A. Stewart and played by members of the Richmond Shepard Mime Theater. From TeleKetics.

The Season

The Season takes a scathingly satirical look at the commercialism of Christmas and the widespread disregard for its symbolic meanings.

In the words of Kevin Thomas of the *Los Angeles Times:* "Mac-Donald intersperses scenes of stinging crassness, of how innocence is relentlessly exploited for a fast buck—the phony-baloney of the department store Santas, the garish irrelevance of the Santa Claus

Lane Parade. He climaxes with two devastating interviews, one with a clod of a Christmas tree salesman . . . and the other with two young men so intelligent they must rationalize their business of supplying real, live Santas for all occasions."

The Season was nominated for an Academy Award and received praise from critics all over the country, including Bosley Crowther of the *New York Times* who called it "a gem."

Since this film is in extremely heavy demand during the Christmas season, it should be booked well in advance. The commercialization of Christmas is significant as a form of the secularization of religious beliefs. It is likewise an example of a value system which places profits above religion. Some viewers will attack the film as unfair, others will have their cynicism confirmed, while still others will appreciate MacDonald's satire.

15 minutes, color, directed by Donald MacDonald (1966). Rental from University of Michigan and Viewfinders.

Seconds to Play

This film could easily have been called "The Making of a Live TV Show," except that Charles Braverman has already claimed that title. *Seconds to Play* is a brief documentary that shows how ABC television goes about covering a football game for national broadcast. The ABC crew arrives five days early to begin set-ups for the prime-time broadcast of the UCLA—Ohio State football game. Camera positions are established, mobile vans arrive and are put into operation, command posts are established, and the thousands of details needed for a national live broadcast are attended to.

The film gives a flavor of the general chaos and also of the amazing coordination needed to bring off what appears to viewers as a smooth-running show. Woody Hayes doesn't want to wait the two minutes needed to bring his team out on cue, and the band gets its signals crossed and remains silent at a crucial time. But the show goes on as the director calls the shots. The hand-held camera picks out the prettiest cheerleader and provides viewers with "color shots." The director admits to being a "dirty old man," explaining that the ABC cameras at sports events always seek out the cheesecake to titillate the male fans across the nation.

Seconds to Play is at least as good as *The Making of a Live TV Show*, although not as slick or tightly edited. Neither film gives a clear picture of all that goes on behind the scenes; for that we may have to wait for Frederick Wiseman to make a film called *TV Director*.

28 minutes, color, directed by Patrick Crowley (1976). From Films Inc.; rental also from Viewfinders.

Seeing Through Commercials: A Children's Guide to TV Advertising

A nasty looking pirate begins this film by telling kids he eats "Pirate Pops" cereal every morning for breakfast because it has "four tasty tropical fruit flavors." But when he eats a spoonful of the cereal on camera, he acts as if he had just bitten down on a rusty doubloon. The director yells "cut," and the pirate removes his eye patch and costume to reveal himself as a friendly actor about to lead young viewers through a guided tour of various types of piratery and skullduggery found on Saturday morning television commercials.

His tour is brief but exceedingly well illustrated and accurate. The first technique he describes is that of making people and products look bigger and better than they are. Products are shown close up, with no context to enable viewers to judge their size accurately. To make things look better than they are, commercials often show kids using a product while having a grand old time. An ad for "Lipsmackers" candy is shown and then repeated with the candy bar replaced by stalks of celery. Vegetables have never looked so good on TV this side of Julia Child.

A fictional ad for a toy called the "Speed Demon Dragster" illustrates how close-ups, camera angles, sound effects, and quick editing can be used to make almost anything look exciting. The same ad is then shown in what could be called an "uncut" version. In this accurate depiction the "dragster" looks like a fine toy for aspiring zombies.

A doll ad for "Little Miss Beauty Pageant" shows how elaborate sets and careful manipulation of the toys can make them appear lifelike.

The pirate-turned-narrator explains that "you have to think about what the words mean" and demonstrates why with an ad for "Sugar Fruit Giggles." He explains that "a bowlful of energy" translates as "filled with sugar," that "with milk to make you strong" means the nutritional value of the cereal is near zero, and "an important part of a nutritious breakfast" again means that the cereal alone is not enough. "Artificial fruit flavors" means that there is no fruit in the cereal.

The film concludes with a commercial for a toy raft. Viewers are asked to discuss it and "find the tricks."

15 minutes, color, directed by Larry Stein and Ruth Ahrens (1976). From Vision Films.

Self-Service

Finally we have a short film that is a worthy successor to the frightful *Jaws.* This time the menacing creature from the animal kingdom is not a killer fish, not a hairy ape with a fetish for tall buildings, not even three-ton, chocolate-covered ants, but a small swarm of nearly invisible mosquitoes. And the human being responsible for the story is not Peter Benchley, but the creative and healthily demented film animator, Bruno Bozzetto.

Self-Service is the story of one man's efforts to defend himself against a bunch of pesky mosquitoes. The victim, however, has that so-common plot device, a tragic flaw. He tends to fall into deep sleep. When he does, the mosquitoes go to work on his body and set up a society that is fueled by their favorite delicacy—human blood. The mosquito society strangely enough resembles human society. There are industrialists, drunks, thieves, and even a Mafia. With all the fun of the road runner versus the fox, the mosquitoes attack and civilize the man's toes, fingers; nose, and whatever else they need. Although they build a thriving, thorough-going self-service culture, the self-service is not necessarily self-serving in the long run because their victim finally lets out a piercing scream and dies. Appropriately, the mosquitoes attend his memorial service.

Self-Service is an entertaining cartoon that would work nicely in theaters as a prelude to any disaster film. But Bozzeto is seldom satisfied with mere entertainment any more than a preacher is satisfied with only passing the collection basket. *Self-Service* is a film about exploitation, about ecology, about using and destroying the source of life itself for passing pleasures or profit. The fact that the doomed exploiters are mosquitoes helps viewers laugh at the comedy, only to feel the sting once they think about and discuss what they have seen.

Self-Service would make an excellent programming combination with *The Fly, Clever Village, The Undoing, Serendipity Bomb*, or even McLaren's *Neighbors*.

11 minutes, color, animation, directed by Bruno Bozzeto. From Connecticut Films.

The Selling of the Pentagon

The Selling of the Pentagon has by now established itself as the most controversial network documentary ever shown on television. Pentagon defenders attacked the film in spite of its unwillingness to accuse the Pentagon of acts far more damning than merely manipulating the news and promulgating a positive public image. The film could have presented Pentagon spokesmen denying the use of crop-killing chemicals in South Vietnam, the burning of villages, the commission of atrocities, the CIA presence in Laos, and domestic military spying.

In spite of its kid gloves approach, the documentary scored heavy blows that American viewers found painful. The viewing audience was told that they spend as much as $190 million a year to have the Pentagon convince them that war is a form of safety precaution, that the Communists have a plan to take over the world, and that the U.S. fights for freedom throughout the globe. Since 1945 the Pentagon has sold the public a bill for 1,100 billion dollars in defense, which includes over 100 billion for Vietnam.

The documentary shows how the "public image" concept has pervaded the military and replaced "the people's right to know." It shows how the "public image" is maintained by impressive weapons displays, by blatantly propagandistic and untrue films for use in schools (the Pentagon film library far exceeds that of almost any commercial distributor), and by a tight control on news released to the media.

The film itself is a form of propaganda even though what it documents is frighteningly true. *The Selling of the Pentagon* is an excellent piece of cinematic journalism and ideal for a study of propaganda, militarism, media control, and freedom of information.

50 minutes, color, directed by Peter Davis. Sale from Carousel Films; rental from University of California, University of Michigan, and Viewfinders.

Serendipity Bomb

Serendipity Bomb is an animated cinema paradox. Into what seems to be a ghost town wanders a traveler. The ghost town, however, turns out to be one very recently deserted. The town is fully furnished; even a phonograph needle still sticks in the final grooves of a scratched record. The empty town becomes a playground for the traveler. He helps himself to a drink at a bar, destroys property, ransacks a museum, contemptuously slops paint all over the hall of justice, pounds on the church organ, and generally fulfills his wildest fantasies.

Meanwhile, on a nearby hill, the town's residents watch through a telescope and try to attract the stranger's attention to warn him of danger. For in the town square lies a huge bomb, the cause of the hurried evacuation. But the stranger ignores their warnings and continues his destructive play. Finally he enters the town bank and carelessly scatters money. This is too much for the residents. They storm back into the endangered village, beat the traveler, and chase him out. But the bomb explodes before they can re-evacuate, and the only survivor is the exiled intruder.

The animation style is superb and the story suspenseful. The film's pure entertainment value is attested by the fact that it was shown last season on *The Great American Dream Machine*. The highly ironic plot is open to many interpretations, all centering on the fact that the people are destroyed in trying to save what they value, while the only person who showed no sense of value was saved.

8 minutes, color, animated, directed by J.F. Laguoionie (1969). From Films Inc. and MMM.

Shaping News for the Consumer

Plaudits to BFA, a subsidiary of CBS, for releasing a film that is critical of TV newscasting. The "message" of *Shaping News for the Consumer* is that news is a commodity shaped to the needs of the consumer. The film recreates the taking of the Roper Poll, which revealed that people depend on and trust television most for their news about the world. A USC professor, who acts as on-camera narrator, points out that these preferences fly in the face of logic, since television is unable to cover ideas adequately.

The main hindrance to TV news is that an average story lasts only 90 seconds, thereby leaving no room for analysis in depth. A TV news producer points out that "we block the shows around the commercials." Eight minutes is allowed for sports and weather, two for opening comments and miscellaneous features, leaving only 30 minutes in an hour for actual news.

The narrator suggests that people should rely on television to stir their interest and give a general idea of what is happening but should not depend on it. In order to be well informed, people must also read magazines and daily newspapers. True, daily papers are 60 to 70 percent advertising, but the reader is free to ignore the ads and still obtain "an awful lot of information."

Shaping News for the Consumer carries a message that seems to be much in need of broadcasting. As long as people admit to depending on TV for most of their news, there is danger of ours becoming a nation of ill-informed citizens.

17 minutes, color. From BFA; rental also from University of California.

The Shopping Bag Lady

Few teenagers really believe that they will someday be old. Oh, they will admit, of course, that they will grow old if they live long enough, but, deep down, the inevitability of this distant event eludes their awareness. There is a corollary to this absence of belief, and that is an unwillingness to accept the fact that old people were once teenagers. Since this lack of faith is assisted by the absence of modern-quality photographs or home movies of grandparents as young people, future generations may find the rigors of aging eased by technology.

At some point in their lives, perhaps at age 14 but often not until much later, young people have an experience that brings home vividly the idea that life is a progression, a journey in which they are traveling on the same road as their parents and grandparents. *The Shopping Bag Lady* is about the initiation of a 14-year-old girl into the knowledge of life as a shared journey.

Emily and her schoolgirl friends walk home through New York's Central Park and come across a "shopping bag lady," one of the countless old women who roam the streets and parks collecting other people's discards and broken dreams. The girls make fun of the old woman; perhaps she is a threat to their vision of life as fun-filled and never-ending. Emily accidentally drops a puppet she made in school, and the old woman adds it to her shopping bag haul for the day. She takes the doll to her "home" under a bridge and reads to it, treating it like a real child.

Later, Emily, a friend, and the friend's little brother visit the Central Park Zoo. The little boy wanders away and meets the old lady. She says hello and begins to show him some of the animals. When Emily's friend sees the two of them together, she calls the police and accuses the old lady of trying to kidnap the boy. Emily testifies to the truth of the trumped-up story, and the old lady is taken away. Afterwards, Emily finds her abandoned shopping bag. She takes it home and pages through an old photograph album that shows a woman named "Annie Lewis" as a young actress, beautiful and full of vitality. She feels a great rush of sympathy for the woman and goes to visit her in the hospital where the police have taken her. Gently, and without saying a word, she communicates her new understanding to Annie. Later that day, she seeks out her own grandmother and begins a new kind of relationship with her.

There is a subtheme in the film dealing with the gulf between wishes and their maturation. Filmmaker Bert Salzman underlines the theme by naming the girl Emily *Carol* and the shopping bag lady Annie *Lewis*. The old lady sums up what is perhaps the deepest meaning of the film as she reads to the puppet a passage from Lewis Carroll's *Alice in Wonderland* where the March Hare chides Alice by saying, "You might just as well say that 'I like what I get' is the same thing as 'I get what I like.' "

The Shopping Bag Lady is a well-directed story film with great audience appeal. Viewers will hopefully see value in it beyond the obvious "Be nice to old people because you too will one day be old."

21 minutes, color, directed by Bert Salzman (1975). From LCA; rental also from MMM.

Silences

Silences is a beautiful film about a gruesome event. Set in German-occupied Yugoslavia in World War II, the film opens as a group of tattered peasants finds the remains of an ambushed German patrol. They strip the corpses of whatever is usable. The husbands and neighbors of these scavengers are the guerrillas who did the killing.

Two peasants begin to strip a soldier and find the young man still alive. They hesitate, torn between their realization that this German is a human being and the knowledge that he is also their enemy. They construct a stretcher and carry him away, only to be confronted by the guerrilla band. The two face their compatriots knowing that their act of kindness is likely to brand them as traitors. One peasant flees in terror, but the other continues his journey carrying the wounded German back to the village. He finds the village in flames, his neighbors and family massacred in reprisal for the ambush. His kindness has now been strained beyond the breaking point; he drags the soldier into the midst of the carnage and clubs him to death.

Silences asks viewers, "What would you do in this situation?" "If you value peace and nonviolence, what is your breaking point?" The film is excellent, both for a discussion of human values and as an example of a fine work of cinema. *Silences* is visually striking with its motifs of fire, flesh, and snow. The film has no narration but uses the language of the eye to speak far more eloquently than any narration ever could.

12 minutes, color, directed by Predrag Golubovic. From McGraw-Hill Films; rental also from University of California and University of Michigan.

Sit Down, Shut Up, or Get Out

This film, a one-hour TV drama shown one Sunday morning on NBC, is similar in theme to the popular *No Reason to Stay*. Both concern the dilemma of survival as an individual in a public school system; both feature a boy named Christopher who is a bright nonconformist.

In Allan Sloane's TV drama the creative rebel, Christopher Bright, is on trial by his teachers and administrators. Teacher-witnesses testify. A math teacher judges him "brilliant, but won't follow the rules," but viewers see in flashback that the teacher merely wants the boy to use his methods even though others might be better. His English teacher also calls him brilliant but "a bad speller, can't capitalize, bad penmanship." As Christopher responds to their unfair charges, the audience comes to see the problem in oversimplified terms—the boy playing the role of the persecuted genius and the school serving as evil fall guy.

The boy's father is supportive, telling him he must "do what you have to do." The father exemplifies a finding by Kenneth Keniston that the "young rebels" are not those reacting against strict parents but those carrying out the values taught them by their more liberal parents. The psychologist is also on Chris's side, but the principal finds the boy a misfit and troublemaker.

Unlike his counterpart in *No Reason to Stay*, Christopher decides to remain at the school if only to "lose on my own terms rather than win on yours."

The ability of this well-performed drama to provoke thought is attested by the more than 1,500 letters NBC received after its first showing.

55 minutes, from Broadcasting and Film Commission, National Council of Churches; rental also from University of California.

The Sixties

Charles Braverman's films (*American Time Capsule, World of '68*, etc.) are popular with high school students, who often request repeat showings. This one is a look at the turbulent 1960s. CBS originally bought the film for around $15,000.00 to use on their "60 Minutes" program. TV producer Don Hewitt claimed that the film "just wasn't very good. It was neither stylish, witty, nor perceptive." Hence, it was cut from the show.

The film is far from a masterpiece, but it *is* stylish and perceptive. The theme of *The Sixties* is polarization, especially as reflected through the influence of George Wallace and Stokely Carmichael. Braverman presents this decade as a time when "right" and "left" became more than the marching orders of obscure political labels. He leaves out many significant events from this period to spare us scenes that we've already witnessed many times over. The result is a sharply honed comment on the times.

15 minutes, color. From Pyramid Films; rental also from University of California, University of Michigan, and Viewfinders.

Sixty Second Spot: The Making of a Television Commercial

This film is not so much about the making of a commercial as it is about the making of a short film. *Sixty Second Spot* hardly acknowledges the existence of the ad agency and instead concentrates on the problems of casting, selecting a location, and shooting with the right lighting and atmosphere. Technically, it is the best of the three shorts on commercials reviewed in this book (*Stalking the Wild Cranberry* and *Buy, Buy, Buy* are the other two), but the one that says least about advertising. *Sixty Second Spot* could just as well be about the making of a scene from a feature film.

The film's subject matter is a 7-Up ad in which a British military commander and his aide trek through Middle Eastern sand dunes to escort a caravan of 7-Up trucks. Their campy conversation makes it clear that British imperialism exists to make the world safe for 7-Up. Although intended as satire, the commercial is not without ironic implications. One wonders what its effect would be if the actors had an American accent, or if one were a Kissinger type.

Sixty Second Spot, like *Stalking the Wild Cranberry*, emphasizes the great pains taken for the best possible footage and presents the filmmakers as dedicated professionals. One of its most fascinating sequences is an audition for the roles of the two leads, in which dozens of actors read the very same lines. As in *Stalking*, the finished commercial is shown at the end of the film.

In sum, *Sixty Second Spot* must be classified as an entertaining and classy film about filmmaking rather than a behind-the-scenes look at the world of advertising. Nice but innocuous.

25 minutes, color. From Pyramid Films; rental also from University of California and Viewfinders.

A Special Report

A Special Report is a satire about the fascination of television news shows with violent death. In it Robert Rancor presents a special report for "Channel Three Moment News" on the brutal murder of Candy Parabola, a 22-year-old topless go-go dancer.

Using all the cliché camera shots and narration of a TV documentary, the report tells how the murder happened as "the curvaceous lady moved quietly in the privacy of her own home." There are the inevitable interviews with a neighbor who says "she was a nice girl," the police inspector who casually says it was "probably just your typical irritations killing," and the reporter's comment that "she is a symptom of the disease of violence."

Each time a new character appears, an identifying tag is superimposed on the screen. CANDY PARABOLA—VICTIM and NEGRO POLICE INSPECTOR are two that make viewers aware of the danger of all-too-neat labels flashed so innocently on the screen.

Since Candy was shot with an arrow, there is an interview with an arrow maker who explains how to obtain that weapon's maximum kill capacity. Since Candy was female, there is a visit to a local karate school where an instructor tells of an influx of women seeking training to protect themselves. One woman interviewed even claims "violence gets too much publicity." The reporter wraps up the special at the side of a tombstone, quoting Shakespeare.

A Special Report is wacky yet incisive. It deals with the dangers involved in TV's handling of crime, its tendency to label and to sound profound while saying nothing. It captures perfectly the ability of a medium to use the guise of public service to play a titillating strip-tease (will they show the corpse?) with a frightened and yet blood-hungry public.

17 minutes, black and white (1970). From USC.

Springman and the SS

Phoenix Films's large collection of the works of Jiri Trnka are of interest to the film historian as well as to aficionados of animation. *Springman and the SS* (originally *Chimney Sweep*) was made by Trnka in 1946 after the Nazi occupation of Czechoslovakia. The two main characters of this political satire are a chimney sweep and an S.S. collaborator. The collaborator's mission is to spy on his neighbors and blow the whistle on any suspicious actions. Although the city is tightly controlled by the S.S. troops and their helpful cohort, their power is jeopardized as soon as the chimney sweep discovers that by attaching springs from a love seat to his feet he can leap over tall buildings with a single bound and thus keep one step ahead of the enemy. In his role as "Springman," he represents the power of the individual to harass his oppressors.

Springman and the SS is action-filled and not without discussion possibilities, but students should be given some background before viewing. In film history courses, *Springman* can be used to illustrate the revolt of early European animators against the impact of Disney, whom they had tended to imitate instead of developing their own style. Disney animation so dominated European markets in the mid-forties, in fact, that any cartoon film was automatically thought of as a "Disney." Stephen Bosustow, an American animator, has called Trnka "the first rebel against Disney's omnipotence."

In *Springman*, Trnka did not use animals to play people; he had people play people. He also used the theme of the common man as a hero instead of the typical Disney preoccupation with the problems of the middle class American.

Trnka made *Springman* when he was 34; it was his last work in cartoon films. He moved into the field of puppet animation and there established himself as a true master.

16 minutes, black and white (1946). From Phoenix Films; rental also from Viewfinders.

Stalking the Wild Cranberry: The Making of a TV Commercial

This film was sponsored by the American Association of Advertising Agencies. As a sponsored film, it is itself an ad for the "dedicated professionals" who make TV commercials. It provides as much behind-scenes nitty-gritty as the oil company ads that portray oil-men as beleaguered conservationists on the side of the little guy and the American Way. In spite of its limitations, however, the film is useful in classes studying TV or advertising.

Stalking the Wild Cranberry presents a condensed version of the making of a Post Grape Nuts commercial in which Euell Gibbons claims he sprinkles wild cranberries on his morning bowl of Grape Nuts. In a series of "re-enacted" conversations among Benton & Bowles agency people, the film shows how a "storyboard" is made and how a multitude of details must be decided upon before the actual shooting. The discussions are so condensed that they appear quite staged and unreal. Using actors who sound like real people would have been better than using real people who sound like actors, and bad actors at that. Nothing is said about money—Gibbons is not "hired"; he is simply "available."

The people who make the commercial are shown as dedicated men who make Herculean efforts to obtain the best possible work. They are also "human" people who can sit around at night after a hard day's filming in the Colorado mountains and joke and play the piano. That ad people are "good guys" seems to be the prime propaganda message of the film.

Stalking does give a few limited insights into the making of a TV commercial: Great effort is expended, many people are involved, and 60 feet of film are thrown away for every foot used.

A topic students often discuss after viewing the film is the credibility of endorsements. Why would a man like Gibbons, supposedly dedicated to natural foods, agree to promote a product of General Foods, an archenemy of the organic food people? I wonder whether Gibbons knows that a vice-president for corporate research at General Foods once said, "We are moving gradually into a world of designed consumer foods. Natural farm produce such as milk, potatoes and grains are no longer just complete foods to be eaten as part of a meal. They have become ever-expanding sources of raw materials to be utilized as building blocks for new and more diverse . . . synthetic foods."

Does the payment of huge fees for endorsements render them all suspect? Can a TV commercial be believed?

Even though *Stalking* is little more than a disguised commercial, it does raise interesting questions and will hold student interest. Recommended with reservations.

14 minutes, color. From Paramount Films; rental also from University of California.

Sticky My Fingers, Fleet My Feet

Sticky My Fingers . . . received an Academy Award nomination in 1970. It was directed by John Hancock, who has since gone on to direct the much acclaimed *Bang the Drum Slowly.* The film, based on a Gene Williams *New Yorker* short story, is scripted by author and drama critic John Lahr. It is a humorous yet revealing look at that time in a man's life when he begins to realize that he will never be a hero and that his adolescent dreams must give way to the realities of age and the younger generation.

Our hero's life centers around touch football games with the guys in Central Park. To his wife he is the perpetual teenager, but in his fantasy world he is a "sticky-fingered antelope," good for six or seven touchdowns a game. He even keeps a private notebook marking every catch and touchdown.

The friendly football game is played by middle-aged men who support each other's fantasies. The homemade gridiron with a trash basket as the goal line is a battlefield where each man can imagine himself a giant and where the real world intrudes only by exception and accident. None of the players has the talent to make third-string water boy on a professional team, but such equality of mediocrity is their bond. Our hero runs more like a drunken aardvark than a fleet antelope, but mere appearances are deceptive, of course.

Sides are chosen in the traditional cruel ritual of acceptance and rejection, which always leaves someone standing alone as the last choice. In this particular game it is a teenaged nephew of one of the players. As the game goes on its Walter Mittyish way, it becomes apparent that the reject is to be the hero and our star receiver his victim. The latter returns home from the muddy defeat imagining himself as an aging superstar who, along with other greats of the sports world, has been forced to realize that "if you live long enough you get old." He tears up his record book, only to be bawled out by his wife as an "immature cripple with pneumonia." But as he falls asleep, she reminds him of his tennis game, and he drifts off, imagining a crowd applauding his backhand.

The acting in *Sticky My Fingers* is excellent, the technical quality and direction far above average, and the entertainment value high. The film presents numerous angles for a discussion of the realization of one's limitations, of sports and heroes, of games as a reflection of society, of middle-age and adolescent dreams and their path through life. If only more people could view this film! It should be televised at half-time on Monday night football.

23 minutes, color. From Time-Life Films; rental also from University of Michigan.

The Stopover

A traveling vagabond emerges from the Greyhound bus luggage compartment and proceeds to use the bus station's pay toilet on someone else's dime. Obviously, our hero is no ordinary hobo or beggar; he is a freeloader *extraordinaire*, a true king of the freebie, and a master of petty thievery.

Dressed as a rather dapper gentleman, he enters a supermarket and prepares for lunch, knowing full well that anything is better than the food at the bus station. But no quick-fingered lifting of a few edibles will do; he takes a cart and first stores a can of Vichyssoise in the cooler. Then he carefully constructs a barrier of cans in his shopping cart to hide what he's up to, breaks out utensils, and starts with a bit of shrimp cocktail for an appetizer and continues with wine and enough food for a banquet. He eats out of the shopping cart, carefully avoiding the curious stares of strangers; but who would think . . .? Satisfied, he leaves the store and makes a legitimate purchase—bromo seltzer.

Some would say this thief is merely doing what his pioneer forefathers did—living off the land. Others would find that this example might lead others to a life of crime. *The Stopover* is surprisingly good for discussion—how practical is the vagabond's life-style, how immoral is it, how could a person enjoy such a life, and what would you do if you had no money?

14 minutes, black and white, directed by Paul Steindl (1975). From Phoenix Films; rental also from Viewfinders.

The Street

We hope there is still room in language arts, literature, and film study programs for a good story well told. *The Street* is a masterful animation of Mordecai Richler's story of a family's reaction to a dying grandmother. The story is a vividly written portrayal of a Jewish family as it waits patiently, somewhat guiltily, for their bed-ridden grandmother to die—"it's for the best." The young boy, who does not yet understand death, waits for his grandma to leave so that he can have a room of his own. *The Street* is a realistic portrayal of death that is far removed from the dozens of films that attempt to present dying as a subject for student discussion. It is not a death-education film, although it will no doubt be used in many schools for that purpose.

The Street is worth showing for the sake of its animation alone. There is no need to justify its use as a "discussion starter" or as a "death-education" film or even as a "film-to-literature" adaptation. Animator Caroline Leaf has made only five previous films and, although only 30 years old, shows a talent and sense of timing that rival the efforts of any animator working today. *The Street*, which took one-and-a-half years to complete, is made with tempera paint mixed with oil and "pushed around" on opal glass. Leaf did the painting under the camera, using a very small field only slightly larger than an index card so that "every little bit of paint moving has more energy when it's blown up on a large screen. And it's less paint to push around, so it goes faster." In Leaf's fluid style, the characters don't

seem to move in a landscape so much as the landscape itself moves to meet and reveal them. Every part of *The Street* is superbly done. The film richly deserved its Grand Prize in the International Animation Festival and the Gold Hugo in Chicago's International Film Festival.

10 minutes, color, animation, directed by Caroline Leaf (1975). From NFBC; rental also from University of California.

Sugar and Spice: A Film About Nonsexist Education

With the growth of the women's liberation movement and the demands for new possibilities for both men and women, there is a need to revise thinking about the roles we teach children to fill. There is a feeling among an increasing number of parents and educators that sex role stereotypes stunt children's growth and limit their capacity to deal with an ever-changing society. *Sugar and Spice* is a film about the attempts of three schools to develop programs that provide role options for both boys and girls.

Part one introduces the issue of stereotyped education and shows the ways sex role divisions are reflected in children's play—boys build block towers and girls serve in support functions. Part two shows a New York City day care center implementing a nonsexist curriculum. Girls are given a chance to feel what it might be like to be a construction worker or firewoman, and both boys and girls participate in cooking lessons. Parts three and four look at attempts in other schools to achieve nonsexist education. In such programs the attitudes of the staff and parents play an important part in the overall curriculum.

Sugar and Spice lacks the sharpness of *Men's Lives* and spends too much time showing talking heads. But the film is valuable for teacher-training classes. It comes with an excellent 27-page discussion guide.

32 minutes, color. From Odeon Films.

Supergoop

Supergoop is an entertaining animated film about the exploitation of children by cereal manufacturers and advertisers, with television serving as accomplice to the crime. "Don't forget, kids, I can make you want things you don't need and never heard of before!" So proclaims Rodney Weatherbottom, a raffish imitation of a hip Tony the Tiger. Rodney spills the Post Toasties on the cereal industry and gives viewers an inside look at just how a new cereal, Supergoop, is created and marketed.

The story begins as a giant cereal conglomerate decides it needs another new product to boost sales. The new cereal is created just like many on the market now—gobs of sugar, a bit of coloring, a sprinkling of vitamins, lots of air for bulk, and last and certainly least, some "cereal that is not so good because the factory has taken most of the food value out!" The name, Supergoop, is invented, and the new product moves to the advertising agency where Rodney is hired to make kids pester their mothers into buying Supergoop. Rodney and Charlie the Adman work together to con the kids by telling them Supergoop will make them big, smart, popular, strong, and have FUN. They decide to put a prize in every box—false teeth—because "the kids'll need them after eating all that sugar."

Charlie the Adman and Rodney come up with some ads that look amazingly like what passes for entertainment on Saturday morning kidvid. As the film ends, some kids who earlier were bugging mom for Supergoop are shown now sick of the new cereal but anxious to try the even newer "Eatum Sweetum." The newer cereal features Rodney, of course, as cartoon spokesanimal.

Supergoop can be used with almost any age level for a study of media images, advertising, nutrition, children's television commercials, or the cereal industry. Is there really such a thing as "Supergoop"? Quaker Oats offers a cereal called King Vitamin, which they claim is "much more than a delicious cereal. It's a multivitamin and iron supplement specially formulated for children and adults alike." Instead of a cartoon tiger on the box, Quaker has a make-believe king. Is the cereal dynamite nutrition? By weight, King Vitamin is 50 percent sugar—supergoop indeed.

In using *Supergoop* with a group, it would be valuable to apply its ideas to other foods, such as snack items, fruit drinks, store bread, and fast food "milk shakes." Compare Rodney the friendly persuader to the army of sales pushers and Supergoop to the tons of pseudo food that line the supermarket shelves.

13 minutes, color, directed by Charles Swenson (1976). From Churchill Films.

Surveillance: Who's Watching?

Surveillance is a 1971 muckraking investigative report on police intelligence activities. Filmmaker Marc Weiss and helpers started out to make a documentary for NET and ended up involved in a Kafkaesque game of investigating the spies who were spying on the investigators. While documenting Chicago police "red squad" activities, the film crew was arrested. What the police didn't know is that one of the crew members was wearing a wireless mike that transmitted every word to a tape recorder. When asked for charges, one of the arresting officers replies, "We'll think of something by the time we get to the station." The crew is eventually booked on suspicion of burglary of their own apartment. Now, two years later, the filmmakers have filed a $250,000 suit charging the police with arrest without probable cause. The plaintiffs also claim that their rights under the first, fourth, fifth, sixth, eighth, ninth, tenth, and fourteenth Amendments were violated.

Such a turn of events imparts drama to the documentary and emphasizes the urgency of the problem of citizen rights. In addition to the scenes of the arrest, there are chaotic shots of police intelligence units at work. The camera crew occasionally confronts the agents at rallies, and the police and filmmakers proceed to take pictures of each other. Much of the film is "talking heads." Sam Ervin makes a few pertinent comments about the right to privacy in his own inimitable way. Counterpoint is provided by Tom Foran, prosecutor of the Chicago Seven, who claims that the idea of "political repression is absolute paranoia." But the paranoia is profitable, as Clyde Wallace, manager of "The Spy Shop," proves as he demonstrates fundamental bugging techniques. The film touches briefly on high school intelligence activities by criticizing guidance counselors who give out private information over the telephone.

The truth of the documentary is at times hard to believe but equally hard to deny.

60 minutes, black and white. From Indiana University.

Sven Nykvist

Sven Nykvist is Ingmar Bergman's cinematographer. In this film he provides a behind-the-scenes look at the making of a Bergman film. It contains excerpts from *Persona, The Shame,* and *Cries and Whispers* and depicts on-set work featuring Liv Ullman and Bergman.

Nykvist explains his theory of making things "to look like they are." He explains that Hollywood films do not do this at all; they tend to produce what he calls a "picture post card look." In lighting scenes, Nykvist strives to avoid all studio lighting even if it means that one-third of a film like *Through a Glass Darkly* has to be shot at sunset or that days must be spent waiting for just the right light to come through a window. Lighting, he says, should present the face as the window to a soul, not by making it beautiful but by showing it to be real and alive. Ullman furthers the comment by comparing the "beautiful hand" used in cosmetic ads with the living hand, each of whose lines tells a story.

"The audience should not be aware that the camera is there. Thirty years and sixty pictures have taught me that the simplest is the best. Now I understand, and that is the most difficult thing."

26 minutes, color, directed by Bayley Sillech (1973). From Films Inc.; rental also from Viewfinders.

Television and Politics

Television and Politics is a 25-minute excerpt from Mike Wallace's CBS-TV show *60 Minutes.* The 1970 film has the high quality that is a *60 Minutes* trademark and a topic that is both timely and crucial.

The film could be named "How to Sell a Candidate" or "Buying Votes with Ads." Political spots are shown beginning with Harry Truman's in 1948, through the clever *March of Time* commercial for Eisenhower in 1952, Nixon's almost legendary "Checker's Speech," Kefauver's use of Eisenhower's own commercials in 1956, the 1960 campaign debates, and finally the ads of Barry Goldwater in 1964 that made the TV spot a lethal weapon. The film clips are damning, revealing, embarrassing, and often humorous.

After tracing the recent history of the political ad, the film switches to interviews with the people who market the candidates. Wallace asks the man who packaged Hubert Humphrey about the morality of a spot in which Agnew is shown on screen and the sound track consists simply of a man laughing. The media man claims to be concerned about politics, not government, and views himself as a "gun for hire."

The economics and morality of TV campaigns are questioned. Agnew's media man says, "We want our candidate to be liked more than understood; we're reaching for the heart rather than the mind."

There are surprisingly frank interviews with political and communications industry people. The film is very much concerned with media morality and even more basically with the Brave New Worldish use of the media in politics.

25 minutes, color. From BFA.

Television: The Anonymous Teacher

Television is a teaching medium, and children absorb its curriculum for an average of three hours daily. In spite of the controversy surrounding the influence of TV on children, few films have been made on the subject. The *Question of Television Violence* is the best, but its one hour length makes it somewhat unwieldy for discussion. United Methodist Communications has produced *Television: The Anonymous Teacher* as a tool for stimulating group interaction among either children or parents on this vital subject.

One of the film's most effective techniques is to show the faces of children as they react to various programs. What they see on the screen is shown in an insert so that we see both the stimulus and the reaction. Two girls fight playfully while watching an ad for Kung Fu GI Joe. We learn that kids don't just "watch" TV; they participate in its pseudo-world.

Various researchers such as ACT's Peggy Charren, Professor Aimee Liefer, Dr. Robert M. Liebert, and others express concern about the dangers of TV. They point out that kids often imitate what they see on the screen, even the commercials, and that they see an enormous amount of adult TV (more children watch on Friday night than on Saturday morning). The critics accuse television of teaching that violence is a socially acceptable way of dealing with problems and that candy, sugar-coated cereal, and toys are very important to health and happiness. They point out that children are taught that men do interesting and usually worthwhile things while women spend a lot of time taking care of men and worrying about good coffee and whiter clothes. They learn from the TV classroom that minority people are less intelligent and less important than white people but are more likely to be funny.

The teaching of television is enormously effective because it works slowly, like erosion. Its effects can be seen only after a period of years, and by then its lessons are too deeply embedded to be easily unlearned.

Television: The Anonymous Teacher comes with an excellent teaching guide.

15 minutes, color (1976). From MMM.

TV News: Behind the Scenes

TV News is a documentary showing how the New York City ABC-TV affiliate puts together its evening "Eyewitness News." The film shows the reporters, editors, writers, and cameramen working smoothly as a team in the exciting job of bringing up-to-the-minute news to the viewing audience. In other words, the film is a nice ABC public relations film. In spite of its PR sheen and superficial approach, however, it does give viewers at least a glimpse behind the scenes at the mysterious process of news gathering.

The film shows a TV reporter on a typical day covering the filming of Shamus, a water main break, and an antiwar demonstration (Geraldo Rivera handles the latter). The film ends with portions of the actual evening news broadcast. Well paced and entertaining, it could be quite useful for courses in mass media on a high school or junior high level. It could be something of an eye opener for viewers in the many cities where local TV news is little more than a wire service rip-and-read process spiced up with film clips provided by the networks, businesses, and the government, plus local pseudo-events like fires.

The teaching guide for *TV News: Behind the Scenes* suggests that the film can be used for career education. If it is so used, someone should point out to viewers that reporters do not meet the likes of Dyan Cannon and Burt Reynolds every day. Thanks largely to Watergate and the "new" journalism, news reporting has become to the 70s what the Peace Corps was to the 60s. Communication educators in high school have done a good job of exciting idealistic students with the potential of journalism for exposing corruption and helping the common man. But the same teachers should warn students that journalism schools are already crammed with far too many students for the available jobs. Enrollment increases of 30 to 40 percent in journalism schools in the mid 1970s were quite common, while the job market expanded little if at all. Use of the film for career education should take these figures into account.

27 minutes, color. From Encyclopaedia Britannica; rental also from University of California and University of Michigan.

Television Newsman

Charles Braverman Productions has released an entertaining, fast-paced look at a day in the life of a large-city TV newsman. Bill Redeker is an "eyewitness reporter" for KABC in Los Angeles. The Braverman team follows Redeker on two stories, one about the financial problems of the Queen Mary, a tourist attraction in Long Beach, and another about the arrest of a large number of illegal aliens at a local factory. Back at the studio, we see Redeker writing the narration, making a voice-over, helping in the editing, timing the film and narration, and finally presenting the story on the evening news. In a voice-over running throughout the film, we hear the views of Redeker on his job and even some criticism of TV journalism.

Television Newsman can be enjoyed simply as an entertaining look behind the scenes of a TV station, and that's all it intends to be. The Braverman group are showmen, not social critics. But the film also stands up for an in-depth discussion of TV news almost in spite of itself. To use the film for this purpose, you have to look between the frames.

Students in large cities will notice that Redeker looks and sounds very much like other "eyewitness" or "action" reporters in their own towns, that his delivery, story format, and even the inflections he uses are much like those of some reporter they see locally.

Viewers will observe that when Redeker arrives at work in the morning, he has no idea what story he will be covering. Such handling of the news ensures coverage by nonexpert reporters, who are seldom able to do more than get the facts straight. Since local newscasts report on relatively few stories each day, stations are not willing to make the expenditure necessary to have reporters stick with certain "beats," which would allow them to observe news in a flow instead of as a series of fragments. The film does not point out this aspect of TV coverage, but the observant viewer will find it nicely illustrated.

The film also shows Redeker "researching" the Queen Mary story and thereby unwittingly points out another disadvantage of TV news. Redeker's "research" seems limited to reading the morning paper and making a few phone calls. Studies have shown that TV stations rely heavily on wire services (national news) and the local paper (local news) for their stories. In spite of all the newsman's efforts, the end product of the evening news is little more than a visual headline service using pictures along with words. Redeker admits that "all we can do is give a feeling for what went on."

He is aware of the evening news as an entertainment vehicle and says, "Sometimes I wonder if we don't try too hard to make every story seem like the end of the world."

Television Newsman is much like a mini-documentary produced by a TV news department. It could be shown to sixth graders, some of whom will come away hoping that they grow up to be TV newsmen, or it could be used in a college journalism course for introduction to a serious discussion of the values and problems of TV news.

28 minutes, color, directed by Charles Braverman (1975). From Pyramid Films; rental also from Viewfinders.

Thank You, M'am

This film adaptation of a popular Langston Hughes short story tells of the confrontation between a purse-snatching ten-year-old and a tough woman nurse with a tender heart. The woman, a night nurse at a city hospital, is on her way home early in the morning. The boy follows her and attempts to grab her pocketbook. But the woman is too big and strong for the boy, and he winds up being towed to her home so that she can wash his face. She drags him along the street admonishing him to behave himself.

The woman knows that the boy needs mothering and nursing more than police action. Instead of anger and revenge she shows sympathy and feeds the boy. He reveals that he wanted her purse in order to buy some shoes. She replies, "You didn't have to snatch my pocketbook to get some shoes—you could have asked me." She gives him 20 dollars and warns him not to steal again because "shoes got that way will burn your feet." The boy walks off with the money and a little love to the good.

Some viewers feel that the woman is dumb, that she should have called the cops. Others feel that the kid will probably spend the 20 dollars on a gun or a knife so that he won't get caught the next time. But most see the woman as a modern Good Samaritan who goes out of her way to provide what others need.

Thank You, M'am is similar in theme to *Martin the Cobbler* but is far more realistic.

12 minutes, color; directed by Andrew Sugerman (1976). From Phoenix Films; rental also from Viewfinders.

They Get Rich from the Poor

They Get Rich from the Poor is a well-made, 28-minute documentary on the relation of organized crime to poverty, a subject desperately in need of exposure. It is made up of the usual combination of interviews and atmosphere shots.

The film contends that the slums have become the "lush territory" of the syndicate, the general proposition of the mob being that "you can make more money in a Harlem than in a Scarsdale." Gambling has been the underground's most lucrative operation since 1920. The rich can go to Las Vegas or the races. But the poor have to settle for mob-controlled numbers rackets and policy games. In one Harlem police precinct, over 22 million dollars is bet in one year.

So what's so bad about gambling? The money the underworld makes from the dimes and quarters of Harlem finances the narcotics operations that help tear ghetto families apart. Organized crime needs slums to stay rich. One black community worker remarks that "no black man brings dope into this country." In one year there were 9500 gambling felony arrests, 32 convictions, and only one prison sentence.

Besides the syndicate's links with dope, gambling, and poverty, the film explores government corruption, nonenforcement of laws, and newspapers that print information useful only in the numbers game. The film might serve to awaken those who believe that poverty in America is an unfortunate accident or the fault of its victims.

28 minutes, color, 1970. From Films Inc.

They Want to Make Work Human Again

This film was originally part of an NBC news "First Tuesday" program. Is assembly line, mechanistic work necessarily alienating? This report, narrated by Edwin Newman, suggests that it is not and that the new techniques of the democratic factory might be the "most significant industrial development since the assembly line."

Swedish automakers Volvo and Saab are shown experimenting with work teams, each held responsible for an entire engine. The Virginia Bell system assigns telephone installers complete responsibility in a specific area rather than making them a part of a general installers pool. The Gaines Dog Food factory has work teams that man the production line, rotate jobs, hire and fire their own members, and use a coworker as team leader, thus eliminating most middle management positions.

The film interviews enthusiastic workers and clearly presents the experiments as a major step toward ending worker boredom and discontent. It makes an excellent companion to *Work*.

17 minutes, color. From Films Inc.; rental also from University of Michigan.

The Things I Cannot Change

". . . the courage to change what I can, the patience to live with the things I cannot change, and the wisdom to tell the difference."

—Plaque on Kenneth Baily's Wall

The National Film Board of Canada's camera crew lived with the Baily family for three weeks to make this amazing documentary about poverty and one family's defense against it. The film does not show how miserable life is without money, but rather how the family lives with being poor. Kenneth Baily works irregularly on the waterfront where he describes life as "dog eat dog." He earned only $1,200 last year. Although he has nine kids and one on the way, which he admits he cannot afford, he continues to have children because he enjoys them and distrusts the pill. Old bread from a local convent, many potatoes that fill the stomach, and lots of love and affection enable the family to survive.

The children all attend school and are not yet completely aware of their handicap; in fact, they seem happier than many youngsters in status-driven suburban families with ten times as much money and ten times fewer members.

Why is Mr. Baily poor? He observes that society is one in which "capitalists capitalize on the poor but the poor never capitalize on the rich." As the film ends, the refrigerator is empty and a new baby has just arrived. All Kenneth Baily can offer is hope and the philosophy reflected by the plaque that hangs on the bare wall.

Be assured that *The Things I Cannot Change* is not the kind of film which attempts to pull heart strings in order to elicit sympathy for the poor.

58 minutes, black and white. From NFBC; rental also from University of California.

This Is Edward R. Murrow

It could be said that Edward R. Murrow was to television news what Disney was to animated film. Murrow was an overriding influence in the 1950s and a weekly visitor to millions of American homes through his program *See It Now* and its spin-off *Person to Person*. He is remembered for his bold exposé of McCarthyism, his hard-hitting documentaries such as *Harvest of Shame*, his interviews with the world's great minds, his pioneer spirit in airing such problems as

school segregation and the link between cigarettes and cancer. In these efforts, Murrow always tried to be objective but was rarely neutral.

This Is Edward R. Murrow traces the career of Murrow from his days as a radio war correspondent to his position as head of the United States Information Agency. Ironically, as USIA chief, Murrow forbade the showing of *Harvest of Shame* in England on the grounds that it gave an unfair impression of the American farmer.

The film, which consists mostly of excerpts from Murrow's programs, presents a fascinating review of some of the events of the 1950s: a lengthy excerpt from Murrow's attack on McCarthy and McCarthy's subsequent rebuttal, for example, and a visit to the apartment of a young senator, John Kennedy, and his wife of only a few days.

Although the film has a 1976 copyright, it is a kinescope of a CBS-TV show probably broadcast after Murrow's death in 1965. It takes the form of a tribute to Murrow rather than an assessment of the man as a shaper of history. But to those studying the history of American television or newscasting, the film should prove valuable. Regrettably, the quality of the image is poor.

44 minutes, black and white. Sale from Carousel Films. Rental from University of California.

To Be a Clown

"To be a clown it is necessary to find the joy in yourself and learn to share that with others. You will find the most difficult skill for a clown is the ability to laugh at yourself." Such precepts are the foundation of a school for clowns run by 27-year-old Richard Pochinko, a man whose physical presence communicates a firm balance between joy and sensitivity.

To Be a Clown sketches the progress of a group of 28 young people as they work intensively to master the art of clowning and overcome their fear of showing emotions before an audience. Pochinko teaches the students the art of self-discovery and guides them in the search for the clown within. His techniques are a cross between theater games and sensitivity training, leading to the creation of a clown face for each person. Students first construct a series of six masks that summarize their whole life experience. They wear the masks, experience them, and finally put the six together to create a seventh mask—the clown face. It is this make-up, this comic mask, that is the most carefully guarded and individual element of the clown's art.

Once students have struggled with the self-discovery process, they are sent out during the lunch hour to perform on the streets, their only mission to make somebody's lunch time happier. The lot of a clown is difficult, for he (or she) desires to overcome the frozen mask of public inexpressiveness by exposing his own mask for public ridicule or acceptance. At the same time, he offers spectators instant identification, for the clown is constantly thwarted, tricked, humiliated, and tromped upon. Audiences can empathize with the infinite vulnerability of a clown and lift their own spirits with the knowledge that he is never defeated; he always springs back for more.

After leaving the school, students join a small circus and we see them clowning before a large audience. After viewing *To Be a Clown*, students will never again view clowns as merely helpless buffoons but will see them as part of the necessary re-creation of the human spirit.

To Be a Clown, well directed by Paul Saltzman, is entertaining, thoughtful, and highly recommended.

34 minutes, color, directed by Paul Saltzman (1974). From Paramount Films.

To Die Today

To Die Today is a documentary presenting the ideas about death and dying of Dr. Elizabeth Kübler-Ross. Dr. Ross spent several years researching the crisis of dying and found that today, more than ever before in history, people are afraid of death. One reason is that with the institutionalizing of the aged and the sick, dying people are out of sight, no longer at home with their families. Because of this estrangement, it is more difficult for them to be comforted or comfortable.

Dr. Ross examines the five emotional stages through which patients generally pass: denial—"it can't be me, there must be a mistake!"; anger—"why me?"; depression; preparatory grief—when feelings of sadness overcome them; and finally, acceptance.

After outlining her theory, Dr. Ross interviews a healthy-looking thirty-year-old man with Hodgkin's disease and a life expectancy of no more than five years. The man betrays no evidence of anger or depression and seems to have reached the state of acceptance. He talks about his past and reveals that he sees his life as one lived richly. After the patient departs, Dr. Ross asks the students present for their evaluation of the patient's seeming acceptance. The students feel that the man is deluding himself in an attempt to cover his real fear. But Dr. Ross explains that they had just seen a rare human being who has had a full life and therefore finds it easier to die with dignity.

To Die Today is truly a moving film about a topic of ultimate importance. The film alone will not help viewers to learn the art of dying, but it will make them aware that death, like life, can be a chance to affirm oneself.

50 minutes, black and white. From Filmmakers Library; rental also from University of California and University of Michigan.

Tomorrow Again

Every day in any large city, the obituary column is filled with the names of the old who were simply too tired to wake for another day. The death certificate will list some purely scientific cause for the end, but those who are in the know are aware that these "causes" are mere excuses. Causes of the death of the aged are rarely clear. Diseases such as loneliness, isolation, and feelings of uselessness never appear in medical reports no matter how much they may be written on the faces of the old.

Grace is an old lady living with other "retired people" in a dreary San Francisco rooming house. In her one-room apartment, she carries out the rituals that define the narrow boundaries of her life. Her dream is to receive attention, praise, recognition. Her tragic flaw is that she is trapped not so much by tired blood and wrinkled skin as by her conception of how to gain affection and her belief in the destructive stereotype of the aged.

She wraps herself in a fur stole and imagines the attention the old men in the lobby will lavish upon her. But in the lobby she is ignored; the old men are more interested in the newspaper and the football game on TV. She imagines herself carried out on a stretcher, thus gaining the attention she so desperately desires. But this is only fantasy and she returns to her room to await another tomorrow.

Director Robert Heath (age 25) has come up with a moving cinematic slice of life that invites an exploration of how to learn to age gracefully, beginning as a teenager. The attitudes students have today about aging help determine how they will act as old people. Although students will not immediately care to consider something as remote (and perhaps frightening) as aging, there is common ground between the two age groups. For both, the future can look bleak and unappealing, and preoccupation with death and nothingness is frequent. Both can pass endless days in doing nothing and feeling there is nothing to do. Both groups are very likely to be self-absorbed, and both alternate between battling for independence and leaning excessively on others.

Tomorrow Again is a simple film and an excellent starting place for a serious consideration of the art of aging.

16 minutes, black and white, 1971. From Pyramid Films; rental also from University of Michigan.

To See or Not to See

To See or Not to See has not gained the popularity it deserves. The National Film Board of Canada production is a humorous and satirical look at the relative values of seeing reality and seeing what one wants to see. Students enjoy the film and cannot easily forget its striking visualization of the inner workings of human perception.

The evolution of a man's perception of the world is traced by using a cartoon character resembling Casper the Ghost to represent his psyche. Throughout the man's childhood, his psyche lives at ease; reality is made to conform to the demands of fantasy and illusion. But at last reality gains strength, and the man suffers what could be called an identity crisis. Having tried drugs and alcohol to no avail, he submits to a doctor's treatment—special glasses that make reality appear to conform to his illusions. All goes well until the patient encounters a steamroller, the danger of which the glasses minimize.

The question remains: Which is more dangerous, the disease or the cure? Should we strive to see things as they are and let the reality overwhelm us, or should we don the glasses of illusion and suffer at the hands of the reality that is then hidden?

15 minutes, color. From LCA; rental also from University of California.

Toys

Toys begins with the innocence of children joyfully viewing a display of toys in a store window. There is a tiger whose jaws open and close, a colorful clown, a scarlet-combed rooster—and there are war toys. The delighted murmurs of the children and the lively musical score stop as, suddenly, a revolving platform of soldiers, rifles, tanks, and planes comes alive. The toys are expertly animated in a battle so real that many viewers feel it in their stomachs. One plastic soldier is burned alive, another is blown to pieces, and "play" napalm plunges from toy planes.

The now still faces of the children are intercut with the plastic faces of the soldiers, and slowly the children come back to life. The music resumes, and the original mood is restored. But one senses that the children are not quite the same; there is some innocence that has been lost; the children and toys have traded places.

Toys prepares children for the real world of adults. The contrast of the innocent children and the ruthless war makes the violence seem even greater, as does the context of a toy display. *Toys* can be used to discuss the influence of war toys, or, on a deeper level, the influence of the games and fantasy world of children on their adulthood. War as a game can be explored, as can the fact that a culture's toys and games often serve as an accurate reflection of its values.

8 minutes, color, directed by Grant Munro (1967). From McGraw-Hill Films; rental also from University of Michigan and Viewfinders.

The Tragedy of the Commons

The Tragedy of the Commons violates one of my unwritten rules for film selection, namely that "the film written for classroom use is the one most likely to be boring and uneducational." *Tragedy* is an exception. It is the kind of film that viewers tend to agree with until the final segment, where they find themselves trapped by logic into debating a position they invariably find abhorrent. For at the end of the film, Dr. Garret Hardin argues persuasively that voluntary birth control is utterly impractical. "We must give up some freedoms or they will be taken from us by natural processes."

Most films on population control settle for the cliché of presenting frightening statistics followed by the simple observation that some form of birth control is needed. *Tragedy of the Commons* goes far beyond that and presents a controversial possibility.

The 23-minute film is in four segments, each with a break for discussion:

1. The common pasture ground of eighteenth-century England is taken as a microcosm for the world. The free pasture became the victim of the profit motive.

2. The difference is shown between a crowded and uncrowded world.

3. The psychology of crowding is explored.

4. The proposal is raised that conscientious people who have only two-child families will not be competitive with people who have no conscience and large families. In other words, if birth control is voluntary, only those without a social conscience will grow in numbers. The proposed solution is "mutual coercion mutually agreed upon."

23 minutes, color. From BFA; rental also from University of California and University of Michigan.

The Trendsetter

The crayon blob hero of *The Trendsetter* is a figure of considerable importance, for when he expresses his tastes and individuality, everyone follows. He buys a uniquely different style of hat and soon everyone is wearing the same kind. He takes up the lost art of pogo stick jumping, and soon the boinging sound of pogo stick enthusiasts in action fills the country. Even something as outrageous as living in the top branches of trees does not deter the mass of people, hungry for any new fad, from following this powerful exemplar. In *The Trendsetter*, Follow the Leader is more than a child's game; it's a way of life.

Finally, our hero devises a scheme to escape his followers. He feigns suicide. True to form, his loyal followers commit suicide. But now there is no one left to follow. A trendsetter without followers is like a hole without a doughnut. His joy gives way to a tear as he views the destruction he has caused and realizes that his phony individuality has meaning only within a crowd.

A common liberal bias about individuality is to state that individuals, people who are different, are punished severely by society.

Since many filmmakers hold the "liberal" outlook on life, there are dozens if not hundreds of films about the nonconformist meeting torture or death or ridicule at the hands of a society which rewards conformity and condemns individuality.

But in *The Trendsetter*, we have a nonconformist who does outrageous things only to be met, not with scorn, but with followers more loyal than any well-trained pet dog. And nothing is more painful to the compulsive nonconformist than a following.

The trendsetter in this film does not fit the description of a free individual. His uniqueness seems to lie in his compulsion to have a following. He is not, appearances to the contrary, a man who "does his own thing," as Ralph Waldo Emerson advised and 100 million people in 1970 professed to do. He is a man who does things, not because he enjoys them, but to prove he is an individual. A real individual does not have to go around proving he is an individual by doing weird things. The free man is sometimes different and sometimes the same but does not expend energy for the sole purpose of being different or being the same. The trendsetter of this film is not a free man in this sense; he is driven by the need to appear different from others.

The crowd in *The Trendsetter* is no more or less free than the trendsetter himself. They are driven by a need to be "in" or "the same" or "up to date." Ultimately, their form of slavery proves fatal. Both the crowd and the trendsetter are more alike than different. Both are lacking in the ability to be what they really are, both play roles, both are enslaved, both are more concerned about how others view them than with self-image, and both are on a road which leads nowhere.

Everyone in the film fails in the primary vocation of life, becoming oneself. Hermann Hesse described it well in the popular novel *Demian*, "Each man had only one genuine vocation—to find the way to himself. He might end up as a poet or madman, as prophet or criminal—that was not his affair, ultimately it was of no concern. His task was to discover his own destiny—not an arbitrary one—and live it out wholly and resolutely within himself. Everything else was only a would-be existence, an attempt at evasion, a flight back to the ideas of the masses, conformity and fear of one's own inwardness." Or, in terms of the film, "Neither a trendsetter nor a follower be, . . . above all, to thine own self be true."

6 minutes, color, animation. From Pyramid Films.

Twins

Twins is the animated story of Lionel and Clifford as seen through the eyes of a psychiatrist who studied both. Although the two boys are twins, their parents have reason to be concerned that they are far from identical. Clifford is reserved and insecure while Lionel is overly zealous and aggressive. To help balance their personalities, the psychiatrist suggests giving Clifford too much for Christmas and Lionel a pile of horse manure. But Cliff finds his overabundance of toys threatening, and Lionel loves shoveling manure day and night.

As often happens to children, they grow up. Timid Clifford somehow joins the army and even earns a medal. Lionel becomes a successful ad man but soon realizes that the public doesn't need most of what he sells. He seeks escape, dropping out to become an organic farmer in New Mexico. Meanwhile, back in the army, Clifford gets shot. Luckily, the half-dollar-size hole completely through his head is only a minor wound, and he escapes from his hospital bed. While wandering around, he meets his long-lost twin brother and the two take to farming together. They sing and dance into the sunset, perhaps to live happily ever after.

Twins is a satire that exists in a moral vacuum. Psychology, parenting, the establishment, dropping out, and even the military are all objects of its barbs. In spite of this ambiguous tone, the film can spark thought and discussion on life-styles or personality. The animation is lively and the action entertaining.

7 minutes, color, directed by Barrie Nelson (1975). From LCA.

The Undoing

In the first shot of this Polish animated film, the screen is filled with cobblestone paving. The camera pulls back to reveal a workman with a wheelbarrow paving everything in sight. The earth he is paving looks alive, like flesh and human innards; the music is "cosmic" and gives his action a universal significance.

He comes to a forest, feels the trees, and continues his paving. Birds fly from the forest into the sun and drop dead on the pavement. Finally, only one tree remains; the camera pulls back to reveal this as the last tree on earth. The man has an awakening as he is confronted with the tree's beauty. He starts to tear up the bricks he has devoted his life to laying down. As he piles up the bricks, the sun is blotted out.

8 minutes, color, animated. From LCA.

Union Maids

Research into the impact of women on American history is a continuing project that many older women can help bring to life by sharing their own experiences. *Union Maids*, a 45-minute documentary by Julia Reichert, James Klein, and Miles Mogulescu, captures the testimony of three aging women who were militant labor organizers in the 1930s. Their stories—oral history at its most animated—are told with extensive historical documentary footage to illustrate the little-known story of the impact of women on American labor history.

The three women—Stella Nowicki, Kate Hundman, and Sylvia Woods—performed unskilled factory work in the early thirties when a woman received 37¢ an hour and a man 52¢. Safety conditions were appalling, and no workmen's compensation existed. Each woman tells of her role in organizing workers, formulating demands, and setting up picket lines in a series of confrontations that ultimately resulted in the formation of labor unions. Despite their activism, which led to jail and firing, none of the women was accorded a job in the union hierarchy.

Union Maids is well paced and both instructive and entertaining. It is another in the string of films needed to correct the impression that U.S. history is the record of a man's world.

45 minutes, color, and black and white, directed by Julia Reichert, James Klein, and Miles Mogulescu (1976). From New Day Films.

The Violin

The Violin is a classic story of two young boys, an old musician, and a violin. The boys save pennies to buy a pawnshop violin, only to find that it produces squeaks and groans instead of music. In disgust they throw the instrument in a trash barrel. An old man sitting nearby retrieves it and coaxes ethereal sounds from the reject. The old musician's magic attracts the boys, and a friendship is formed, based on learning the mastery of the violin. The trio enjoys the companionship until suddenly the old man loads his belongings into a boat and prepares to leave. In his haste to bid good-bye, one boy falls on the violin, crushing it. But the old man gives him his own beautiful violin as a way of passing on a part of himself. The boy stands on the shore playing a sad farewell while the old man rows away.

The Violin is a beautifully made film with each shot composed, lighted, and colored to stir the viewers' memories. For example, the colors are muted and primary colors are almost totally avoided to add to the film-as-memory effect. The feature film, *Fiddler on the Roof*, uses the same technique to evoke the past.

The film has the mood of a sentimental violin, moving those viewers willing to be influenced by sentiment and the beauty of music. Adults are most affected by the film's sentimentality; many remember an old man in their childhood who gave them a gift that has lasted. Those teenagers who break into laughter at the sound of a violin will find the film only boring. Others with the ability to be easily moved will find *The Violin* emotional to the point of tears.

25 minutes, color, directed by George Pastic (1972). From LCA; rental also from University of California and University of Michigan.

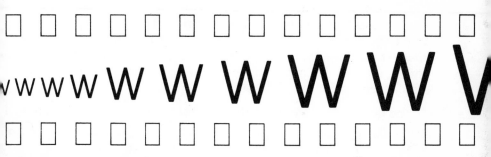

Waiting for Fidel

If the fictional Godot had ever shown up, Samuel Beckett's play likely would never have become a classic. It is equally fortunate that when the National Film Board of Canada sent Michael Rubbo and two compatriots to Cuba to film an interview with Fidel Castro, the Premier failed to show. Instead of a dull interview, we have a film about the conflict between social systems as mirrored in the trio thrust into a strange land, waiting for some Godot to make sense of it all.

Michael Rubbo is the NFBC filmmaker; Joey Smallwood is a Canadian politician who calls himself a socialist; and Geoff Stirling, the money behind the operation, is a self-made media baron and millionaire. They jet into Cuba for the interview and are told that they will have to wait a day or two. While they are waiting for Fidel, they visit revolutionary Cuba and try to make sense, each in his own terms, of what they see. At Lenin High School they find tuition and room and board completely free, but students must spend 16 hours a week working at making baseballs or radios. Stirling calls the school a sweatshop. Smallwood wishes that every student in Canada could spend some time working with his hands. Rubbo explains that the Cubans can't afford to give their children nonproductive years; schools have to pay for themselves.

A visit to a mental hospital increases the tension among the three visitors. Each sees the same things but translates them according to his own background. At the mental hospital, success is measured by a decline in population, and work therapy seems the main form of help offered. The trio argues constantly about what human nature is, and a woman inmate (is she crazy or perceptive?) explains to the trio that greatness is defined in terms of ability to help others.

They visit an apartment project where the rent is 6 percent of the breadwinner's salary and the construction workers are amateurs, and also a university where students are paid to study. Each encounter with a new approach to organizing society is a challenge for them to defend or attack. Finally, the society of three is split by arguments. Fidel is unable to keep his promise for the interview, and the group heads back with enough footage to make one of the most intriguing "documentaries" to come along in years.

Waiting for Fidel is a source of endless discussion possibilities about the structure of society, about socialism versus capitalism, about the perception of society based on one's own preconceptions, and even about the nature of documentary filmmaking. Highly recommended for mature audiences.

58 minutes, color, directed by Michael Rubbo. From Open Circle Cinema.

The Wall

The Wall is another devastating animation parable from the Zagreb Film Studio in Yugoslavia. The hero of this four-minute short is an urbane, derby-hatted man who, in the course of his travels, is confronted by a high and seemingly endless brick wall.

He steps aside as another traveler comes along and attempts to get over the wall. He tries to climb it, jump over it, pole-vault over it, but each effort fails. Frustrated, he leaves the wall and heads off in a different direction. A third man comes along with his own techniques for getting over the wall. The presence of the original man, calmly watching all the activity, makes his repeated failures even more frustrating. Finally, in desperation, he throws himself full speed at the wall and crashes through. He is destroyed in the process, but there is a hole in the wall. The original man tips his hat and walks through the opening. On the other side of the wall is another wall, equally high and long. He sits down and waits for someone else to come along and do his work.

Some will see the film's main character simply as the most intelligent of the three. Why not have others do your work? Some will see him as a personification of the people-user, who reaps without sowing. Discussion can begin by asking what the wall symbolizes and what kind of person each of the three men represents.

4 minutes, animation, color, directed by Ante Zaninovic (1965). From International Film Bureau; rental also from University of Michigan.

Watch Your Step

A paunchy, middle-aged victim of life enters a deserted New York subway corridor. He struggles to carry an old vacuum cleaner with its multitude of tubes and attachments, a large black suitcase, and a baseball glove. The man's girth and baggage turn the simple task of riding up the escalator into a Sisyphean project. Add to his problems the obsession with picking up a stray dime, plus the fact that the escalator leads nowhere, and viewers are in for a masterful example of the humor of frustration. Parts of this struggle of human beings versus the stubborn world of unyielding inanimate objects rank well against the best of Chaplin and other masters of silent comedy. But the comedy of struggle is only a backdrop for allegory.

Watch Your Step is meant to be analyzed and dissected until every symbol has been laid out on the table of explication. The hero is everyperson trapped by his or her dreams and possessions. The escalator is a means of escape as well as the treadmill of modern life, the dime a distraction from more cosmic goals, and so on and so on.

Watch Your Step is well directed by Theodore Page and can be enjoyed by viewers who don't know a symbol from a dill pickle. Those who enjoy the search for allegory can learn as much about life from taking apart the pieces of the film as biology students can learn about animals from dissecting a frog. A full-length study guide helps in explicating, or discussing, the film. It hardly ranks with the world's most powerful allegories, but it can teach the concept of things as symbols.

Perhaps the "everyperson" really represents the filmmaker himself, burdened as he is with the need to give every object and action symbolic weight. The escalator then symbolizes the endless discussion going nowhere that the film can generate. With a hungry audience and skilled discussers, the film offers a fruitful exercise in interpretation; with any audience, it should provide at least a few laughs and some memorable moments of empathy.

12 minutes, color, animated (1975). From Xerox Films.

We Call Them Killers

They are intelligent with highly developed senses. They can enjoy the tickle of a feather or the quiet beauty of a flute. They are more obedient than many teenagers and watch films with undivided attention. Their hearing is exquisite, and their ability to entertain is attested by thousands who have seen them perform. In spite of these virtues, we call them killers. But one close look at the double row of razor teeth in each of these two-ton creatures explains why "killer whale" is not an unrealistic name.

Dr. Paul Spong is Canada's answer to John Lily and a man who believes that killer whales could someday participate in interspecies communication. It is human beings who must first overcome their fear, which acts as the principal barrier to communication. In other words, it's not easy to talk to someone who might turn you into a meal. As Spong places his head in the jaws of a whale, he explains that this gesture says to the whale, "I am, I trust you." So far, the whales have understood.

The first third of the film shows two whales at Sealand of the Pacific performing the usual gamut of whale/dolphin tricks. The sequence is included both to entertain viewers and to point out the irony of using these animals as a tourist attraction instead of as means to explore interspecies communication. Dr. Spong's experiments suggest that the whales respond to music, and flutist Paul Horn is brought poolside to demonstrate the whale's empathy. Perhaps music transcends not only the language barrier but also the species barrier.

We Call Them Killers is a brief, superficial look at the possibility that animals might have something to say to humans.

Produced by the National Film Board of Canada (1973). From NFBC; rental also from University of California.

Weekend

Weekend is a live-action film from the Zagreb studios that proposes a rather startling answer to the question, "How should the old be allowed to die?"

As the film begins, a family is preparing for a picnic in the country. They handle their grandfather like a fragile knickknack. His favorite old rocker is carefully tied to the roof of the car, and the family leaves the city. The chair on top of the tiny European car is a strange sight as it passes through the city, but it is also symbolic of the living and the dying. The city itself is like the car–chair, a combination of the new and the old, the fast-moving urban center and the reminders of ages long dead.

The picnic is a quiet, relaxing affair. The mood changes suddenly to one of sorrow as the family movingly says goodbye to their grandfather. They show signs that this is a permanent parting. The family drives away leaving grandfather sitting contented and noble on his chair in the open fields. Slowly the camera reveals he is not alone; scattered throughout the fields are other old people also quietly sitting and waiting.

The film is unresolved yet powerful in impact. The method of death chosen is both cruel and dignified.

12 minutes, color, directed by Ante Zaninovíc. From MMM; rental also from University of Michigan.

What on Earth

"Two-thirds of the land encompassed by the city of Los Angeles is covered by freeways and roads and streets and parking lots and gasoline stations and automobile salesrooms and private garages and other appurtenances of automobiling."

—Denis Hayes

"You are what you drive" runs an ad for a sports car. Autos play such an important part in our lives that a visitor from outer space might have a hard time telling who controls the planet—cars or people.

In *What on Earth*, Martians send a photographic exploration team to orbit earth. In the format of a movie newsreel, the Martian narrator explains to the homefolks what earth is like. The only problem is that the Martians have concluded, not without reason, that the real inhabitants of the planet are the automobiles. Gas stations become restaurants, rush hour is explained by noting that earthlings have a "compulsive desire to play together," garages are medical centers, road signs and billboards are seen as education. But, the narrator asks, "What is his ultimate purpose?" The answer is found in the junkyard (retirement park) where the "mature individual makes his essential contribution to his civilization." Here the individual is taken and changed, then returned to a "breeding" center to contribute to the creation of yet another individual—a unique sexless reproduction system.

The main problem encountered by earthlings is the huge hives (cities) which slow down the citizens. But, the narrator assures us, a top priority task is the removal of these hives (urban renewal).

The film is useful for a study of the role of the automobile in our society, how values and even the pace of living are shaped by the auto,

how it influences life-style. It's great fun to watch and an excellent starting place for a unit questioning the automobile as a benefit to civilization.

10 minutes, color, animation, directed by Les Drew and Kaj Pindal. From McGraw-Hill Films.

What Teacher Expects . . . The Self-Fulfilling Prophecy

This National Film Board of Canada film is about exactly the same topic as CRM's *Productivity and the Self-Fulfilling Prophecy*. The advantage of the NFBC film is that it limits its concern to the classroom; its disadvantage is that it lacks the dazzle and polish of the CRM film.

Rosenthal (see the review of the CRM film) appears in this film, and some experiments with teaching children words are shown. Teachers are confronted with the fact that they fulfilled their own expectations in the teaching experiment.

What Teacher Expects proposes the most interesting application of the self-fulfilling prophecy by asking: Do hospital patients die sooner if doctors expect them to die?

26 minutes, black and white. From NFBC.

Where All Things Belong

Where All Things Belong is a highly professional, up-beat, inspirational film about the theme of renewal, rebirth, and the human capacity for change.

After a contemplative introduction consisting mainly of nature shots set to a rather weak folk song, the theme of renascence, of rebirth, is introduced by an Indian walking along a beach. He explains, "To the Red Man, all things share the same breath, all things are connected." His ancient insight is reinforced by NASA photos of earth taken from outer space—the simple act of seeing these photos has changed us all. They confirm visually what our inner being has told us all along—all is one.

Author George Leonard appears in the film, explaining how running (as opposed to racing) is a process of rebirth. He is also shown demonstrating Aikido, a sport/art that is "a single act with no winner and no loser."

The film moves quickly, illustrating the wide scope of rebirth by allowing creative individuals to comment on their own capacity to change and create—a poet, a sculptor, a mountain climber. The joys of hang gliding, playing with children, and even the act of childbirth itself are presented in beautifully filmed sequences. The natural childbirth sequence is pure joy and the ultimate summary of the film's theme.

In some ways the film resembles *Why Man Creates*. Both deal with a very wide-ranging, yet specific subject matter; both use a combination of interviews and nonnarrated segments to hint at answers to larger questions.

Where All Things Belong is a film more for inspiration than study, a beautiful film with a universal message.

28 minutes, color, produced as a pilot for a possible television series, made by Dick Gilbert, Bob Samples, James Halpin, Skeets McGrew, Joern Gerdts, and David Altschul (1975). From Essentia Productions.

Where Did Leonard Harry Go?

Leonard Harry was a plain and undistinguished little man who held a humdrum job in a humdrum factory and lived with an equally humdrum wife. Leonard, the narrator explains, was very unhappy and often wished he were someone or something else. One day he began experimenting with fantasies and became very good at imagining that he was a big movie star or a little old lady. He became so good at disguise that he lost his job at Toil, Inc.; his boss was quite tired of having him show up for work one day as an elephant and the next as a palm tree. But Leonard didn't care because at last life was exciting.

Mrs. Harry became frantic; she never knew if Leonard was her bed or her broom. But never mind; he had become such a master of fantasy that he never again was himself. Until this day Mrs. Harry is never sure of what he is. The narrator surmises that Leonard probably became something else, perhaps a flower pot or a hat rack. Leonard is still around, still plain, and still undistinguished.

Where Did Leonard Harry Go? is animated in an appropriately humdrum style and could serve as a children's film or an introduction or discussion starter for any age level on the topics of self-identity, fantasy, and the art of being other than what we are.

7 minutes, color, animated, directed by William Van Horn (1975). From Xerox Films.

Whistling Smith

Whistling Smith is a NFBC production nominated for a 1975 Academy Award in the category of Documentary Short Subjects. Sgt. Bernie Smith is a foot patrolman in Vancouver, Canada's "tenderloin district." He deals with the prostitutes, pimps, junkies, or just plain vagrants on the basis that "policemen are street people too." But Whistling Smith is no heroic father figure or humanitarian counsellor. He is a bit of the petulant king disturbed that criminals show up in "his" kingdom and also a bit of the tough drill sergeant faced with shaping up raw recruits the city throws his way. He cajoles street-walkers, pushes aside loiterers, confiscates glue bags, and bad mouths the "street people" who clutter the sidewalks and storefronts on his beat.

His approach is not well received by the police department, is not completely legal, and does not conform to the latest thinking on police methods. But whatever the street people feel about Smith, they all seem to fear and respect him. Since he makes it difficult to be a street criminal, the crime rate on his beat has been cut in half. The question remains, however, whether Smith has actually cut crime or merely moved it off his beat and down the street a few blocks.

The film is made in a style befitting its subject—rough, mobile, always moving, fragmented. At times, *Whistling Smith* resembles a Fred Wiseman film; the camera follows Smith and shows what happens on his beat. The faces of the criminals are often blacked out, but their language and reactions to Smith always come through. The film is nonjudgmental about his techniques and produces a surprising amount of disagreement and discussion in almost any viewing audience. *Whistling Smith* acts as a catalyst for evaluating one's own belief in human nature. Viewers cannot discuss the film without also revealing their view of the evil or goodness of human nature.

Whistling Smith has a wide variety of uses in value education, social studies, or even film making. It is a vital film that can energize a class or adult audience.

27 minutes, color (1975). From Wombat Productions.

Who Invited Us?

Who Invited Us? is a one-hour NET documentary that caused much controversy when shown on TV. Many stations refused to carry the program, the educational channel in Washington included.

The documentary traces the history of American foreign policy from 1918 to the present, focusing on military intervention. The viewpoint of the film is that most of the intervention is based on a basic conflict between capitalism and socialism, which dates back to 1918, when we sent 10,000 troops to aid the French in Siberia after the Russian Revolution. We failed, and one-sixth of the world was closed to American economic interests. Since then we have intervened when it was to our "best interests"—Cuba, Dominican Republic, Iran (CIA), Greece, Guatemala, Mexico, Honduras, Haiti, Chile, Philippines, Columbia, and Bolivia among others. In theory, we do not support dictatorships; in practice, this policy applies only to Cuba.

60 minutes, black and white, 1970. From Indiana University; rental also from University of Michigan.

A Wonderful Construction

A Wonderful Construction is a poetic eulogy to construction workers. It contrasts the reality of disgruntled hard hats working for a buck with a vision of construction workers as craftsmen capable of changing the world. Director Don Lenzer uses poetic narration, interviews with workers, and the paintings and ideas of Fernand Léger for a cinematic study of the reality versus the vision.

Lenzer interviews the workers at a "USA all the way" street rally. He is hopelessly out of touch with these men but presses on, asking questions that the workers had never thought of: "Why do you do what you do?" "What are your dreams?" "What would you do if money were no problem?" No worker interviewed reveals any expansive hidden dreams. All work to get by and because the pay is good even though they hate the work.

Lenzer is not satisfied with their answers; he sees more. "I've learned a secret that many of you don't know. There is behind you the creative force of your work. You are craftsmen capable of changing the world." He presents the ideas and paintings of Fernand Léger, who saw the entire city aflame with color and major political struggles fought over the color of a building. He saw builders as secure men who could control their own lives and manage their own work, unafraid of their neighbors and themselves, men with the courage to pursue their dreams.

But Léger is dead, and his paintings decorate the walls of the rich and hang in museums. His vision of a gigantic circus where work and play intermix is yet to be born. People have stopped watching again, and the buildings continue to build themselves.

15 minutes, color. From Film Images.

Work

Work is a documentary about the alienation created by assembly line work. The film opens with a closeup of the huge Goodyear sign in Detroit that ticks off the minute-by-minute car production of that city. The total at the time of filming (1970) was 5,748,653. The camera then enters the factory to examine just how these cars are manufactured. The focus is on the production line, which moves with a force beyond the control of any one human worker. The line worker is reduced to being an extension of the machine; having to adjust his movements to the movements of conveyor belts, he becomes just another interchangeable part of the factory.

The only narration is provided by occasional quotes from Karl Marx, unfortunately not the sort to endear the film to suburban high school students. The narrated quotes point out that "In handicraft the worker makes use of the tool. On the assembly line, the tool uses the worker." And, "Alienating work is that which represents not the satisfaction of a need, but the means of satisfaction of other needs. The work does not belong to the worker. If man is alienated from his labor he will also be alienated from others."

There are a few interviews with assembly line workers and a brief scene in a custom car shop where work is more personal and presumably nonalienating. But the message of the film comes not from the interviews or even the quotes of Karl Marx. The message is in the scenes of the ever-moving assembly line where it becomes difficult to tell where the machine leaves off and the man begins.

Work is excellent for a discussion of the nature of work, alienation, "careers," and social change. In its brief 15 minutes, it offers no alternatives but does pose some questions that even Detroit workers are asking with increasingly strident voices.

15 minutes, color (1970). From Tricontinental Film Center.

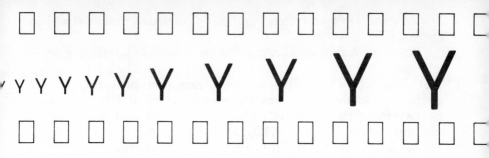

You, Irresistible You

An accurate title for this film would be *Four Short Skits by the Inimitable Marshall Efron.* Many viewers will remember Efron from the ill-fated *Great American Dream Machine* on Public Television, where he demonstrated how to make lemon cream pie without lemons or cream. For those unfamiliar with Efron, simply conjure up an image of a cross between Ralph Nader and Julia Child.

His first skit takes on male cosmetics. He demonstrates the mushrooming product line which includes *Thicket* (makes hair look thicker), *Other* (a deodorant crotch spray), a bronzer, a foot spray, and other sundries that are part of the master plan for the total man.

Next, he takes on waterbeds and sets out to investigate the claim that "two things are better on a waterbed." He finds instead that a waterbed advertised for $20 can cost hundreds of dollars with all the needed and desired options—especially if that "other" is to be better.

The third segment moves from waterbeds to the 58-million-dollar market in tanners. Finally, Efron marches to his podium with a stack of research reports to answer the burning question, "Is there sex after death?" His report is predictably brief.

11 minutes, color. From Benchmark Films; rental also from Viewfinders.

Young Man with a Future

Peter Foldes is a Frenchman who ranked as one of the most creative and distinctive film animators before his early death from cancer in 1977. His name is probably not well known among film educators because of the obtuse, gruesome, and pessimistic nature of his films. But his work should be viewed if only for an appreciation of his unique metamorphosis technique of animation. Images in a Foldes film slowly dissolve and shift from, say, a person to a rocket, or a baby into a person into two separate individuals. Each metamorphosis reveals new and often frightening potentials that exist within everyone.

Thus, in *Young Man with a Future*, a mother nurses her baby, who grows in her arms into a boy who devours her. The boy becomes a grotesque man, who strangles, chews, tears, and shoots hundreds of people in a bloody killing spree. He becomes a tank and then a cannon as the screen fills with medals. Finally, he turns into an atomic bomb standing triumphant over a Dantesque sea of the dead.

Women come to offer him their bodies and crown him with a laurel wreath. He spurns them, but when he discovers a phonograph, he is reduced to tears at the sound of classical music. A woman approaches to offer solace, and they embrace in a rare show of tenderness. The peace, however, is short-lived, for a hussy attracts him; he squeezes her and out fall a dozen babies. The sexual conquest again triggers his blood lust, and he strides across the screen killing left and right until he meets his master.

Young Man with a Future is the most accessible of all the Foldes films. His animation style is utterly unforgettable even if his message is filled with contradictions and a disturbing love/hate attitude toward women. Foldes is not easy to take, but neither are many true artists.

7 minutes, color, animation. From Films Inc.; rental also from Viewfinders.

ZZZZZZZ Z Z Z Z Z

Zen and Now

Zen and Now is an Alan Watts rap on some aspects of an Eastern life-view that Westerners could use to regain their collective sanity. The visual content of the film consists entirely of nature shots of one huge garden; the idea is that one need not travel around the world to see a universe. Watts's slow, sparse narration carries the film. Some verbatim and paraphrased samples from the script:

"The great problem of civilization is to come back to your senses. People confuse what comes in by their senses with words and symbols by which they are described. The real world can never be defined; it is the 'unspeakable world.' Things don't exist; the world is a multidimensional network of vibrations. As we grow up we're told what vibrations are good and what are bad. Growing up means becoming prejudiced. Even having a fever isn't necessarily dreadful. Most people in our culture would rather have money than wealth."

"If I talk all the time I could never hear what anyone says. If I think all the time I will have nothing to think except thought. Hence the importance of Zen meditation—stop thinking altogether and be aware of what is. Don't name anything. Allow light and sound to play with your senses. There is no past, no future, only now."

About five minutes of the film contain no narration and allow the viewers a brief taste of nonthinking meditation.

14 minutes, color. From Hartley Productions.

ADDRESSES OF DISTRIBUTORS

Action for Children's Television (ACT), 46 Austin St., Newtonville,
    MA   02160
Agency for Instructional Television (AIT), Box A, Bloomington,
    IN   47401
Alternatives on Film, P.O. Box 22141, San Francisco, CA   94122
Arthur Mokin Productions, 17 West 60th St., New York,
    NY   10023
Benchmark Films, 145 Scarborough Rd., Briarcliff Manor,
    NY   10510
BFA Educational Media, 2211 Michigan Ave., Santa Monica,
    CA   90406
Billy Budd Films, 235 E. 57th St., New York, NY   10022
Brigham Young University, Dept. of Motion Picture Production,
    Provo, UT   84602
Carousel Films, 1501 Broadway, New York, NY   10036
Creative Film Society (CFS), 7237 Canby Ave., Reseda, CA   91335
Churchill Films, 662 N. Robertson Blvd., Los Angeles, CA   90069
Connecticut Films, 6 Cobble Hill Rd., Westport, CT   06880
Counterpoint Films, 14622 Lanark St., Panorama City,
    CA   91402
Encyclopaedia Britannica Educational Corp. (EBE), 425 N.
    Michigan Ave., Chicago, IL   60611
Essentia Productions, P.O. Box 129, Tiburon, CA   94920
Film Images, 17 West 60th St., New York, NY   10023
Filmmakers Library, Inc., 290 West End Ave., New York,
    NY   10023
Filmwright, 4530 18th St., San Francisco, CA   94114
Films for the Humanities, Box 378, Princeton, NJ   08540
Films Inc., 1144 Wilmette Ave., Wilmette, IL   60091
Green Mountain Post Films, P.O. Box 177, Montague, MA   01351
Hartley Productions, Cat Rock Rd., Cos Cob, CT   06807
International Film Bureau (IFB), 332 S. Michigan Ave., Chicago,
    IL   60604
Images, 2 Purdy Ave., Rye, NY   10580
Indiana University, Audio-Visual Center, Bloomington, IN   47401
John Howard Association, Children in Trouble Project, 67 East
    Madison St., Suite 1216, Chicago, IL   60605

Learning Corporation of America (LCA), 1350 Ave. of the
    Americas, New York, NY   10019
McGraw-Hill Films (MGH), 1221 Ave. of the Americas, New York,
    NY   10020
Macmillan Audio Brandon, 35 MacQuesten Parkway South, Mount
    Vernon, NY   10550
Mass Media Ministries (MMM), 2116 N. Charles St., Baltimore,
    MD   21218
Motivational Media, 1001 N. Poinsettia Place, Hollywood,
    CA   90046
National Council of Churches, Communication Commission, 475
    Riverside Drive, Room 860, New York, NY   10027
New Day Films, P.O. Box 315, Franklin Lakes, NJ   07417
New Line Cinema Corp., 853 Broadway, New York, NY   10003
New York University Film Library, 26 Washington Place, New York,
    NY   10003
New Yorker Films, 43 West 61 St., New York, NY   10023
National Film Board of Canada (NFBC), 16th Floor, 1251 Ave. of
    the Americas, New York, NY   10020
Northwestern University Film Library, Box 1665, Evanston,
    IL   60201
Odeon Films, 1619 Broadway, New York, NY   10019
Open Circle Cinema, P.O. Box 315, Franklin Lakes, NJ   07417
Paramount Communications, 5451 Marathon St., Hollywood,
    CA   90038
Perspective Films, 369 West Erie St., Chicago, IL   60610
Phoenix Films, 470 Park Ave. South, New York, NY   10016
Pyramid Films, Box 1048, Santa Monica, CA   90406
Ralph Arlyck Films, 79 Raymond Avenue, Poughkeepsie,
    NY   12601
RBC Films, 933 North La Brea Ave., Los Angeles, CA   90038
Serious Business Company, 1145 Mandana Blvd., Oakland,
    CA 94610
Silo Cinema, P.O. Box 315, Franklin Lakes, NJ 07417
Soho Cinema, 225 Lafayette St., New York, NY   10012
Stephen Bosustow Productions, 1649 11 St., Santa Monica,
    CA   90404
TeleKetics, 1229 S. Santee St., Los Angeles, CA   90015
Texture Films, 1600 Broadway, New York, NY   10019
Time-Life Films, 100 Eisenhower Drive, Paramus, NJ   07652
Tricontinental Film Center, 333 Ave. of the Americas, New York,
    NY   10014
University of California, Extension Media Center, 2223 Fulton St.,
    Berkeley, CA   94720

University of Michigan, Audio Visual Education Center, 416
  Fourth St., Ann Arbor, MI   48103
University of Southern California (USC), Division of Cinema, Film
  Distribution Section, University Park, Los Angeles,
  CA   90007
Viewfinders, Box 1665, Evanston, IL   60201
Vision Films, P.O. Box 48896, Los Angeles, CA   90048
Vision Quest, 7715 N. Sheridan Rd., Chicago, IL   60626
Western World Productions, P.O. Box 3594, San Francisco,
  CA   94119
Wombat Productions, Little Lake, Glendale Rd., Ossining,
  NY   10562
Xerox Films, 245 Long Hill Rd., Middletown, CT   06457

SUBJECT INDEX

The subject listing that follows is intended to serve as a source of creative inspiration for film selection, programming, and course planning. Use the index to add variety to your film selection much as you might use a thesaurus to add life to word selection in writing.

The film topics are only suggestions; they do not indicate that a film was made for the purpose of shedding light on the topic listed.